# Federal Benefits

for Veterans,
Dependents and
Survivors

**VA** | U.S. Department
of Veterans Affairs

vets.gov

2016 Edition

# Phone Numbers

Bereavement Counseling...............................................1-202-461-6530
Civilian Health and Medical Program (CHAMPVA)..........1-800-733-8387
Caregiver Support ......................................... 1-855-260-3274
Debt Management Center.......................................1-800-827-0648
Education..........................................................1-888-442-4551
Foreign Medical Program...........................................1-888-820-1756
Headstones and Markers...............................................1-800-697-6947
Health Care......................................................1-877-222-8387
Homeless Veterans...........................................1-877-424-3838
Home Loans......................................................1-888-827-3702
Life Insurance..................................................1-800-669-8477
National Cemetery Scheduling Office.............................1-800-535-1117
Pension Management Center.......................................1-877-294-6380
Presidential Memorial Certificate Program....................1-202-565-4964
Telecommunication Device for the Deaf (TDD)..............1-800-829-4833
VA Benefits......................................................1-800-827-1000
VA Combat Call Center .............................................1-877-927-8387
Veterans Crisis Line...........................................1-800-273-8255
Women Veterans...........................................1-877-222-8387

## Web Sites

Burial and Memorial Benefits .........................................www.cem.va.gov
Caregiver Support ........................................ www.caregiver.va.gov
CHAMPVA............www.va.gov/hac/forbeneficiaries/forbeneficiaries.asp
eBenefits......................................................www.ebenefits.va.gov
Education Benefits...........................................www.gibill.va.gov
Environmental Exposures...............www.publichealth.va.gov/exposures
Federal Recovery Coordination Program .............. www.va.gov/icbc/frcp
Health Care Eligibility....................................www.va.gov/healthbenefits
Homeless Veterans..................................... www.va.gov/homeless
Home Loan Guaranty....................................www.homeloans.va.gov
Life Insurance.........................................................www.insurance.va.gov
Memorial Certificate .Program........................www.cem.va.gov/pmc.asp
Mental Health................................................www.mentalhealth.va.gov
My HealtheVet....................................................www.myhealth.va.gov
National Resource Directory .............................................www.nrd.gov
Records.........................www.archives.gov/st-louis/military-personnel
Returning Servicemembers....................................www.oefoif.va.gov
State Departments of Veterans Affairs......www.va.gov/statedva.htm
Women Veterans...........................................www.womenshealth.va.gov
VA Vet Centers...............................................www.vetcenter.va.gov
VA Home Page.......................................................www.va.gov
VA Benefit Payment Rates........................www.vba.va.gov/bln/21/rates
VA Forms........................................................www.va.gov/vaform

# Introduction

Veterans of the United States Armed Forces may be eligible for a broad range of benefits and services provided by the U.S. Department of Veterans Affairs (VA). These benefits are codified in Title 38 of the United States Code. This booklet contains the most commonly requested VA benefits and services.

This booklet is a brief overview of the commonly sought information concerning Veterans Benefits. For the most accurate information, Veterans and family members should visit the websites provided within this publication as regulations, payments, and eligibility requirements are subject to change. For additional information, please visit www.va.gov.

To find the nearest VA facility, go to www.va.gov/directory/guide/division.asp?dnum=1&isFlash=0 or call 1-800-827-1000.

**General Eligibility:** Eligibility for most VA benefits is based upon discharge from active military service under other than dishonorable conditions. Active service means full-time service, other than active duty for training, as a member of the Army, Navy, Air Force, Marine Corps, Coast Guard, or as a commissioned officer of the Public Health Service, Environmental Science Services Administration, or National Oceanic and Atmospheric Administration or its predecessor, the Coast and Geodetic Survey. Dishonorable and bad conduct discharges issued by general courts-martial may bar VA benefits. Veterans in prison must contact VA to determine eligibility. VA benefits will not be provided to any Veteran or dependent wanted for an outstanding felony warrant.

**Important Documents:** In order to expedite benefits delivery, Veterans seeking a VA benefit for the first time must submit a copy of their service discharge form (DD Form214, DD Form 215, or for World War II Veterans, a WD form).

## eBenefits

**Through eBenefits Veterans can:** Apply for benefits, view their disability compensation claim status, access official military personnel documents (e.g., DD Form 214, *Certificate of Release or Discharge from Active Duty*), transfer entitlement of Post-9/11 GI Bill benefits to eligible dependents (Servicemembers only), obtain a VA-guaranteed home loan Certificate of Eligibility, register for and update direct deposit information for certain benefits, and search for employment through the Veterans Employment Center (VEC). New features are added regularly.

**Accessing eBenefits:** The portal is located at www.ebenefits. va.gov. Servicemembers or Veterans must register for an eBenefits account at one of two levels: basic or premium. A premium account allows the user to access personal data in VA and Department of Defense (DoD) systems, as well as apply for benefits online, check the status of claims, and more. The basic account limits the self-service features that can be accessed.

To register for an account, Veterans must be listed in the Defense Enrollment Eligibility Reporting System (DEERS) and obtain a DoD Self Service (DS) Logon. Servicemembers can access eBenefits with a DS Logon or common access card (CAC). They can choose from two levels of registration: DS Logon level 1 (basic) and DS Logon level 2 (Premium). A DS Logon is an identity (user name and password) that is used by various DoD and VA Websites, including eBenefits. Those registered in DEERS are eligible for a DS Logon. A DS Logon is valid for the rest of the Servicemember's life.

Identity verification: Many people will be able to verify their identity online by answering a few security questions. A few may need to visit a VA regional office or TRICARE Service Center to have their identities verified. Servicemembers may verify their identity online by using their CAC. Military retirees may verify their identity online using their Defense Finance and Accounting Service (DFAS) logon. Veterans in receipt of VA benefits via direct deposit may have their identity verified by calling 1-800-827-1000 and selecting option 7.

## Contents

# Health Care Benefits

For additional information on VA health care, visit: www.va.gov/ health as well as **V**HA's 2015 Health Care Benefits Overview, a guide designed to provide Veterans and their families with the information they need to understand VA's health care system.

**Basic Eligibility:** A person who served in the active military, naval, or air service and who was discharged or released under conditions other than dishonorable may qualify for VA health care benefits including qualifying Reserve and National Guard members.

**Minimum Duty Requirements:** Veterans who enlisted after Sept. 7, 1980, or who entered active duty after Oct. 16, 1981, must have served 24 continuous months or the full period for which they were called to active duty in order to be eligible. This minimum duty requirement may not apply to Veterans discharged for hardship, early out, or a disability incurred or aggravated in the line of duty.

**Enrollment:** For most Veterans, entry into the VA health care system begins by applying for enrollment. Veterans can now apply and submit their application (VA Form 1010EZ), online at www.va.gov/va-forms/form_detail.asp?formno=10ez. If assistance is needed for the online enrollment form, an online chat representative is available to answer questions Monday – Friday, between 8 a.m. and 8 p.m. EST. Veterans can also enroll by calling 1-877-222-8387, Monday through Friday, 8 a.m. to 8 p.m. EST, or at any VA health care facility or VA regional office. Once enrolled, Veterans can receive health care at VA health care facilities anywhere in the country.

The following four categories of Veterans are not required to enroll, but are urged to do so to permit better planning of health resources:
1. Veterans with a service-connected disability of 50 percent or more.

2. Veterans seeking care for a disability the military determined was incurred or aggravated in the line of duty, but which VA has not yet rated, within 12 months of discharge.

3. Veterans seeking care for a service-connected disability only.

4. Veterans seeking registry examinations (Ionizing Radiation, Agent Orange, Gulf War/Operation Enduring Freedom/Operation

Iraqi Freedom/Operation New Dawn (OEF/OIF/OND) depleted uranium, airborne hazards and Airborne Hazards and Open Burn Pit Registry).

**Priority Groups:** During enrollment, each Veteran is assigned to a priority group. VA uses priority groups to balance demand for VA health care enrollment with resources. Changes in available resources may reduce the number of priority groups VA can enroll. If this occurs, VA will publicize the changes and notify affected enrollees. A description of priority groups follows:

**Group 1:** Veterans with service-connected disabilities rated 50 percent or more and/or Veterans determined by VA to be unemployable due to service-connected conditions.

**Group 2:** Veterans with service-connected disabilities rated 30 or 40 percent.

**Group 3:** Veterans who are former prisoners of war (POWs).
Veterans awarded the Purple Heart medal.
Veterans awarded the Medal of Honor.
Veterans whose discharge was for a disability incurred or aggravated in the line of duty.
Veterans with VA service-connected disabilities rated 10 percent or 20 percent.
Veterans awarded special eligibility classification under Title 38, U.S.C., § 1151, "benefits for individuals disabled by treatment or vocational rehabilitation."

**Group 4:** Veterans receiving increased compensation or pension based
on their need for regular aid and attendance or by reason of being permanently housebound.
Veterans determined by VA to be catastrophically disabled.

**Group 5:** Nonservice-connected Veterans and noncompensable service-
connected Veterans rated 0 percent, whose annual income and/or net worth are not greater than VA financial thresholds.
Veterans receiving VA Pension benefits.
Veterans eligible for Medicaid benefits.

**Group 6:** Compensable 0 percent service-connected Veterans.
Veterans exposed to ionizing radiation during atmospheric testing or during the occupation of Hiroshima and Nagasaki.
Project 112/SHAD participants.
Veterans who served in the Republic of Vietnam between Jan. 9, 1962 and May 7, 1975.

Veterans who served in the Southwest Asia theater of operations from Aug. 2, 1990, through Nov. 11, 1998.
Veterans who served in a theater of combat operations after Nov. 11, 1998, as follows:
Veterans discharged from active duty on or after Jan. 28, 2003, for five years post discharge;
Veterans who served on active duty at Camp Lejeune, N.C., for no
fewer than 30 days beginning Aug. 1, 1953, and ending Dec. 31, 1987.
**Group 7:** Veterans with incomes below the geographic means test income
thresholds and who agree to pay the applicable copayment.
**Group 8:** Veterans with gross household incomes above VA national income threshold and the geographically-adjusted income threshold for their resident location and who agree to pay copayments. Veterans eligible for enrollment: Noncompensable 0-percent service-connected:
**Subpriority a:** Enrolled as of Jan. 16, 2003, and who have remained enrolled since that date and/or placed in this subpriority due to changed eligibility status.
**Subpriority b:** Enrolled on or after June 15, 2009, whose income exceeds the current VA national income thresholds or VA national geographic income thresholds by 10 percent or less Veterans eligible for enrollment: nonservice-connected and
**Subpriority c:** Enrolled as of Jan. 16, 2003, and who remained enrolled since that date and/ or placed in this subpriority due to changed eligibility status.
**Subpriority d:** Enrolled on or after June 15, 2009 whose income exceeds the current VA national income thresholds or VA national geographic income thresholds by 10 percent or less.

Veterans NOT eligible for enrollment: Veterans not meeting the criteria above:
**Subpriority e:** Noncompensable 0-percent service-connected.
**Subpriority f:** Nonservice-connected.
VA's income thresholds change annually and current levels can be located at: http://nationalincomelimits.vaftl.us/.

## Veterans Choice Program
As directed by the Veterans Access, Choice and Accountability Act of 2014, VA implemented the Veterans Choice Program, which will

operate for 3 years or until the Fund is exhausted. The program allows certain eligible Veterans to elect to receive care from non-VA health care providers if they cannot receive VA care within 30 days or live more than 40 miles from a VA facility or face excessive travel burdens.

VA will also extend the Assisted Living Pilot Program for Veterans with Traumatic Brain Injury for 3 years, through October 6, 2017. This program assesses the effectiveness of providing assisted living services to eligible Veterans with traumatic brain injuries to "enhance the rehabilitation, quality of life, and community integration of such Veterans."

Under the Act, Veterans can receive counseling and appropriate care and services required to overcome psychological trauma resulting from military sexual trauma (MST) that occurred while the Veteran was serving on inactive duty training (such as drill weekends for members of the Reserves and National Guard). Such benefits are provided at no cost to the Veteran.

The Choice Act also authorizes VA, in consultation with the Department of Defense (DoD), to provide MST-related care and services to members of the Armed Forces on active duty (including members of the National Guard and Reserves) without the need for a referral from a TRICARE provider or a military treatment facility. VA is working with DoD on implementation of this benefit.

**Women Veterans:** Women Veterans are eligible for the same VA benefits as male Veterans. Comprehensive health services are available to women Veterans including primary care, specialty care, mental health care, residential treatment and reproductive health care services. VA provides management of acute and chronic illnesses, preventive care, contraceptive and gynecology services, menopause management, and cancer screenings, including pap smears and mammograms. Maternity care is covered in the Medical Benefits package. Women Veterans can receive maternity care from an OB/GYN, family practitioner, or certified nurse midwife who provides pregnancy care. VA covers the costs of care for newborn children of women Veterans for seven days after birth. Infertility evaluation and limited treatments are also available. Women Veterans Program Managers are available at all VA facilities to assist women Veterans in their health care and benefits. For more information, visit <u>www.wo-</u>

menshealth.va.gov or call the Women Veteran Call Center at 1-855-VA Women (1-855-829-6636)

**Lesbian Gay Bisexual and Transgender (LGBT) Veterans:** LGBT Veterans are eligible for the same VA benefits as any other Veteran and will be treated in a welcoming environment. Transgender Veterans will be treated based upon their self-identified gender, including room assignments in residential and inpatient settings. Same-Sex Couples: VA launched a new website to inform Veterans and beneficiaries of the recent changes in the law and procedures involving same-sex marriages. Veterans can learn more about VA's guidance regarding same-sex marriages at www.va.gov/opa/marriage.

**Military Sexual Trauma:** Military sexual trauma (MST) is the term that VA uses to refer to sexual assault or repeated, threatening sexual harassment that occurred while a Veteran was serving on active duty (or active duty for training if the service was in the National Guard or Reserve). VA health care professionals provide counseling and treatment to help Veterans overcome health issues related to MST. Veterans who report experiences of MST but who are deemed ineligible for other VA health care benefits or enrollment, may be provided MST-related care only. For additional information, visit: www.mentalhealth.va.gov/msthome.asp.

**Presumptive Eligibility for Psychosis and Other Mental Illness:** Certain Veterans who experienced psychosis or other mental illness within a specified timeframe will have their psychosis presumed to be service-connected for purposes of VA medical benefits.

**Psychosis:** Eligibility for treatment of psychosis, and such condition is exempted from copayments for any Veteran who served in the United States active duty military, naval, or air service and developed such psychosis within two years after discharge or release from the active military duty, naval or air service; and before the following date associated with the war or conflict in which the Veteran served: Mental Illness (other than Psychosis): Eligibility for benefits is established for treatment of an active mental illness (other than psychosis), and such condition is exempted from copayments for any Veteran of the Persian Gulf War who developed such mental illness:
1.  Within two years after discharge or release from the active duty military, naval, or air service; and

2. Before the end of the two-year period beginning on the last day of the Persian Gulf War (end date not yet determined).

**OEF/OIF/OND Care Management:** Each VA medical center has an Operation Enduring Freedom/Operation Iraqi Freedom/Operation New Dawn (OEF/OIF/OND) Care Management team in place to coordinate patient care activities and ensure that Servicemembers and Veterans are receiving patient-centered, integrated care and benefits. More information for connecting with OEF/OIF/OND Care Management teams can be found at www.oefoif.va.gov.

Key Information for Veterans about the Affordable Care Act /Health Care Law
- Veterans who are enrolled in VA health care don't need to take additional steps to meet the health care law coverage standards.

- The health care law does not change VA health benefits or Veterans' out-of-pocket costs.

- Veterans who are not enrolled in VA health care can apply at any time.

For additional information about VA and the health care law, visit www.va.gov/aca or call 1-877-222-VETS (8387).

**Financial Assessment:** Most Veterans not receiving VA disability compensation or pension payments must provide a financial assessment, also known as a means test, upon initial application to determine whether they are below VA income thresholds. VA is currently not enrolling new applicants who decline to provide financial information unless they have a special eligibility factor exempting them from disclosure. VA's income thresholds are located at http://nationalincomelimits.vaftl.us/.
As of 2014, VA no longer requires enrolled non-service connected and 0-percent non-compensable service connected Veterans to provide their financial information annually. A means test will continue to be collected from Veterans at the time of application for enrollment. In lieu of the annual financial reporting, VA will confirm the Veteran's financial information using information obtained from the Internal Revenue Service and Social Security Administration.

**Medical Services and Medication Copayments:** Some Veterans are required to make copayments (copays) to receive VA health care

7

and/or medications. For more information on the specific rates for Inpatient, Extended Care, Outpatient and Medication copayments please see Fact Sheet IB 10-430, "Copay Rates" at the following VA link: www.va.gov/healthbenefits/resources/publications.asp.

**NOTE:** Copays apply to prescription and over-the-counter medications, such as aspirin,aspirin; cough syrup or vitamins dispensed by a VA pharmacy. Copays are not charged for medical supplies, such as syringes or alcohol wipes. Copays do not apply to condoms. Health Savings Accounts: (HSAs) can be utilized to make VA copayments. HSAs are usually linked to High Deductible Health Plans (HDHPs).

**Private Health Insurance Billing:** VA is required to bill private health insurance providers for medical care, supplies and medications provided for treatment of Veterans' nonservice-connected conditions. Generally, VA cannot bill Medicare but can bill Medicare supplemental health insurance and/or TRICARE for Life (TFL) for covered services. VA is authorized to bill and accept reimbursement from High Deductible Health Plans (HDHPs) for care provided for nonservice-connected conditions.VA may also accept reimbursement from Health Reimbursement Arrangements (HRAs) for care provided for nonservice-connected conditions.

**Reimbursement of Travel Costs:** Eligible Veterans and non-veterans may be provided mileage reimbursement or, when medically indicated, special mode transport (e.g., wheelchair van, ambulance), when travel is in relation to VA medical care. Mileage reimbursement is 41.5 cents per mile and is subject to a deductible of $3 for each one-way trip and $6 for a round trip; with a maximum deductible of $18 or the amount after six one-way trips (whichever occurs first) per calendar month. The deductible may be waived when travel is; in relation to a VA compensation or pension examination; by a special mode of transportation; by an eligible non-veteran; or will cause a severe financial hardship, as defined by current regulatory guidelines.

**Eligibility:** The following are eligible for VA travel benefits:
- Veterans rated 30 percent or more service-connected.

- Veterans traveling for treatment of service-connected conditions.

- Veterans who receive a VA pension.

- Veterans traveling for scheduled compensation or pension examinations.

- Veterans whose income does not exceed the maximum annual VA pension rate.

- Veterans in certain emergency situations

- Veterans whose medical condition requires a special mode of transportation and travel is pre-authorized (Advanced authorization is not required in an emergency, and a delay would be hazardous to life or health).

- Certain non-veterans when related to care of a Veteran (caregivers, attendants, donors, and other claimants subject to current regulatory guidelines)

**Reporting Fraud:** Help VA's Secretary ensure integrity by reporting suspected fraud, waste, or abuse in VA programs or operations. Report fraud to:

**VA Inspector General Hotline**
810 Vermont Avenue, N.W.
Washington, D.C. 20420
E-mail: vaoighotline@va.gov
VAOIG hotline: (800) 488-8244
Fax: (202) 495-5861

**Veteran Health Registries:** Certain Veterans can participate in a VA health registry and receive free evaluations. VA maintains health registries to provide special health evaluations and health-related information. To participate, contact the Environmental Health Coordinator at the nearest VA health care facility or visit http://www.publichealth. va.gov/exposures to see a directory which lists Environmental Health Coordinators by state and U.S. territory. Veterans should be aware that a health registry evaluation is not a disability compensation exam. A registry evaluation does not start a claim for compensation and is not required for any VA benefits.

**Gulf War Registry:** For Veterans who served on active military duty in Southwest Asia during the Gulf War, which began in 1990 and continues to the present, and includes Operation Iraqi Freedom

(OIF) and Operation New Dawn (OND).

**Embedded Fragment Registry:** OEF, OIF, and OND Veterans who have or likely have an embedded fragment as the result of an injury they received while serving in an area of conflict.

**Agent Orange Registry:** Agent Orange is an herbicide that the U.S. military used between 1962 and 1971, during the Vietnam War, to remove jungle that provided enemy cover. Veterans serving in Vietnam were possibly exposed to Agent Orange or its dioxin contaminant. Veterans eligible for this registry evaluation are those who served on the ground in Vietnam between Jan. 9, 1962, and May 7, 1975, regardless of the length of service; this includes Veterans who served aboard boats that operated on inland waterways ("Brown Water Navy") or who made brief visits ashore. Information is also available through VA's Special Issues Helpline at 1-800-749-8387.

**Ionizing Radiation Registry:** For Veterans who have received nasopharyngeal (nose and throat) radium irradiation treatments while on active duty and Veterans possibly exposed to radiation.

**Airborne Hazards and Open Burn Pit Registry:** Unlike other registries, when Veterans complete the online Airborne Hazards and Open Burn Pit Registry self-assessment questionnaire, they are in the registry. No in-person medical evaluation is required to become registered. Veterans not already enrolled in VA health care should contact an Environmental Health Coordinator at a nearby VA facility by visiting the following link: (http://www.publichealth.va.gov/exposures/coordinators.asp) or calling 1-877-222-8387.

**Vet Center Readjustment Counseling Services:** VA provides readjustment counseling services, to include direct counseling, outreach, and referral, through 300 community-based Vet Centers located in all 50 states, the District of Columbia, Guam, Puerto Rico, and American Samoa. Vet Center counselors provide individual, group, marriage, and family readjustment counseling to those individuals that have served in combat zones or areas of hostilities. Counselors assist in making a successful transition from military to civilian life; through treatment for posttraumatic stress disorder (PTSD) and help with any other military-related problems that affect functioning within the family, work, school or other areas of everyday life. Other psycho-social services available include outreach, education, medical referral, homeless Veteran services, employment, VA benefit referral, and the brokering of non-VA services.

**Bereavement Counseling related to Servicemembers:** Bereavement counseling is available through VA's Vet Centers to all immediate family members (including spouses, children, parents, and siblings) of Servicemembers who die while serving on active service. Vet Center bereavement services for surviving family members of Servicemembers may be accessed by calling (202) 461-6530. For additional information, contact the nearest Vet Center, listed in the back of this book, or visit www.vetcenter.va.gov.

**Vet Center Combat Call Center:** 1-877-WAR-VETS is an around the clock confidential call center where combat Veterans and their families can call to talk about their military experience or any other issue they are facing in their readjustment to civilian life. The staff is comprised of combat Veterans from several eras as well as family members of combat Veterans.

**Home Improvements and Structural Alterations:** VA provides up to $6,800 lifetime benefits for service-connected Veterans/Servicemembers and up to $2,000 lifetime benefits for nonservice-connected Veterans to make home improvements and/or structural changes necessary for the continuation of treatment or for disability access to the Veterans'/Servicemembers' home and essential lavatory and sanitary facilities. For application information, contact the Prosthetic Representative at the nearest VA medical center.

**Special Eligibility Programs:** VA provides comprehensive health care benefits, including outpatient, inpatient, pharmacy, prosthetics, medical equipment, and supplies for certain Korea and Vietnam Veterans' birth children diagnosed with spina bifida (except spina bifida occulta).

**Services for Blind and Visually Impaired Veterans:** Severely disabled blind Veterans may be eligible for case management services at a VA medical center and for admission to an inpatient or outpatient VA blind or vision rehabilitation program.

**Mental Health Care Treatment:** Veterans eligible for VA medical care may receive general and specialty mental health treatment as needed. Mental health services are available in primary care clinics (including Home Based Primary Care), general and specialty mental health outpatient clinics, inpatient mental health units, residential rehabilitation and treatment programs, specialty medical clinics, and Community Living Centers. For more information on VA mental health services, visit www.mentalhealth.va.gov/VAMentalHealth-Group.asp.

**Veterans Crisis Line:** Veterans experiencing emotional distress/crisis, or who need to talk to a trained mental health professional, may call the Veterans Crisis Line, 1-800-273-TALK (8255). The hotline is available 24 hours a day, seven days a week. When callers press "1," they are immediately connected with a qualified and caring provider who can help.

**Chat feature:** Veterans Chat is located at www.veteranscrisisline.net and by clicking on the Veterans chat tab on the right side of the webpage.

**Text feature:** Those in crisis may text 83-8255 free of charge to receive confidential, personal, and immediate support. European access: Veterans and members of the military community in Europe may dial 0800-1273-8255 or DSN 118. For more information about VA's suicide prevention program, visit: www.mentalhealth.va.gov/suicide_prevention/.

**The PTSD Coach** is a mobile application that provides information about PTSD, self-assessment, and symptom management tools and information about how to connect with resources that are available for those who might be dealing with post-trauma effects. The PTSD Coach is available as a free download for iPhone or Android devices.

**Outpatient Dental Treatment:** Dental benefits are provided by VA according to law. In some instances, VA is authorized to provide extensive dental care, while in other cases treatment may be limited by law. For more information about eligibility for VA medical and dental benefits, contact VA at 1-877-222-8387, or www.va.gov/healthbenefits.

**Vocational and Work Assistance Programs**
**VHA Therapeutic & Supported Employment Services (TSES) Programs**: These programs are designed to assist Veterans with living and working as independently as possible in their respective

communities. Participation in TSES vocational services cannot be used to deny or discontinue VA disability benefits. Payments received from Compensated Work Therapy Sheltered Workshop and Transitional Work and Incentive Therapy cannot be used to deny or discontinue SSI and/or SSDI payments and are not subject to IRS taxes.

**Long-term Care Services:** VA provides institution-based services (nursing home level of care) to Veterans through three national programs: VA owned and operated Community Living Centers (CLC), State Veterans' Homes owned and operated by the states, and the community nursing home program. Each program has admission and eligibility criteria specific to the program. VA is obligated to pay the full cost of nursing home services for enrolled Veterans who need nursing home care for a service-connected disability, or Veterans or who have a 70-percent or greater service-connected disability and Veterans with a rating of total disability based on individual unemployability. VA will provide nursing home care for all other Veterans based on available resources.

**Emergency Medical Care in U.S. Non-VA Facilities:** In the case of medical emergencies, VA may reimburse or pay for emergency non-VA medical care not previously authorized that is provided to certain eligible Veterans when VA or other federal facilities are not feasibly available. This benefit may be dependent upon other conditions, such as notification to VA, the nature of treatment sought, the status of the Veteran, the presence of other health care insurance, and third party liability. Because there are different regulatory requirements that may affect VA payment and Veteran liability for the cost of care, it is very important that the nearest VA medical facility to where emergency services are furnished be notified as soon as possible after emergency treatment is sought.

**Foreign Medical Program:** VA may authorize reimbursement for medical services for service-connected disabilities or any disability associated with and found to be aggravating a service-connected disability for those Veterans living or traveling outside the United States. Veterans calling from within the Philippines may contact the VA office in Pasay City at 1-800-1888-8782. If calling from outside of the Philippines, the number is 011-632-318-8387. Veterans may also register by email at IRIS.va.gov. All other Veterans living or planning to travel outside the U.S. should register with the Foreign

Medical Program, P.O. Box 469061, Denver, CO 80246-9061, USA; telephone 303-331-7590. For information, visit: www.va.gov/hac/for-beneficiaries/fmp/fmp.asp.

**Caregiver Programs and Services:** VA has long supported family caregivers as vital partners in providing care worthy of the sacrifices of America's Veterans and Servicemembers. Each VA medical center has a Caregiver Support Program coordinated by a Caregiver Support Coordinator (CSC). The CSC coordinates caregiver activities and serves as a resource expert for Veterans, their families, and VA providers.

## Non-Health Care Benefits

**Disability Compensation**: Disability compensation is a tax-free monetary benefit paid to Veterans with disabilities that are the result of a disease or injury incurred or aggravated during active military service. The benefit amount is graduated according to the degree of the Veteran's disability on a scale from 10 percent to 100 percent (in increments of 10 percent). Compensation may also be paid for disabilities that are considered related or secondary to disabilities occurring in service and for disabilities presumed to be related to circumstances of military service, even though they may arise after service. To be eligible for compensation, the Veteran must have been separated or discharged under conditions other than dishonorable.

The payment of military retirement pay, disability severance pay and separation payments, such as Special Separation Benefit (SSB), Reservists' Involuntary Separation Pay (RISP), and Voluntary Separation Pay (VSP) may affect the amount of VA compensation paid to disabled Veterans.

Veterans with disability ratings of at least 30 percent are eligible for additional allowances for dependents, including spouses, minor children, children between the ages of 18 and 23 who are attending school, children who are permanently incapable of self-support because of a disability arising before age 18, and dependent parents. The additional amount depends on the disability rating and the number of dependents.

Monthly disability compensation varies with the degree of disability and the number of eligible dependents. Disability compensation benefits are not subject to Federal or state income tax. Detailed compensation rate information can be found at www.benefits.va.gov/compensation/rates-index.asp

**Special Monthly Compensation (SMC)**: SMC is an additional tax-free benefit that can be paid to Veterans as well as their spouses, surviving spouses, and parents. For Veterans, SMC is a higher rate of compensation paid, due to special circumstances such as the need for aid and attendance by another person, or due to a specific disability such as the loss of use of one hand or leg. A Veteran who is determined by VA to be in need of the regular aid and attendance of another person, or a Veteran who is permanently housebound, may be entitled to additional payments.

## 2015 VA Disability Compensation with no dependents

| Disability Rating | Monthly Rate |
|---|---|
| 10 percent | $133.17 |
| 20 percent | $263.23 |
| 30 percent* | $407.75 |
| 40 percent* | $587.36 |
| 50 percent* | $836.13 |
| 60 percent* | $1,059.09 |
| 70 percent* | $1,334.71 |
| 80 percent* | $1,551.48 |
| 90 percent* | $1,743.48 |
| 100 percent* | $2,906.83 |

## 2015 VA Disability Compensation with a spouse

| Disability Rating | Monthly Rate |
|---|---|
| 10 percent | $133.17 |
| 20 percent | $263.23 |
| 30 percent* | $455.75 |
| 40 percent* | $651.36 |
| 50 percent* | $917.13 |
| 60 percent* | $1,156.09 |
| 70 percent* | $1,447.71 |
| 80 percent* | $1,680.48 |
| 90 percent* | $1,888.48 |
| 100 percent* | $3,068.90 |

A Veteran evaluated at 30 percent or more disabled is entitled to receive an additional payment for a spouse who is in need of the aid and attendance of another person. Comprehensive rate information and detailed instructions on calculating benefits can be found: www.benefits.va.gov/COMPENSATION/resources-rates-read-compAnd-SMC.asp.

**Automobile Allowance**: As of Oct. 1, 2013, Veterans and Service-members may be eligible for a one-time payment of not more than $20,114.34 toward the purchase of an automobile or other conveyance if they have service-connected loss or permanent loss of use of one or both hands or feet, or permanent impairment of vision of both eyes to a certain degree.

**Clothing Allowance**: Veterans who have unique clothing needs as a result of a service-related disability or injury may receive a supplement to their disability compensation. The clothing allowance reimburses Veterans whose clothing gets permanently damaged by a prosthetic or orthopedic appliance they wear, or by a prescribed medication used on their skin. Eligible Veterans receive a one-time or yearly allowance for reimbursement. To apply, contact the prosthetic representative at the nearest VA medical center. Current rates can be found at: www.benefits.va.gov/COMPENSATION/special_Benefit_Allowances_2014.asp.

**Additional Benefits for Eligible Military Retirees**: Concurrent Retirement and Disability Pay (CRDP) is a DoD program that allows some individuals to receive both military retired pay and VA disability compensation. Normally, such concurrent receipt is prohibited. Veterans do not need to apply for this benefit, as payment is coordinated between VA and the military pay center. To qualify for CRDP, Veterans must have a VA service-connected disability rating of 50 percent or greater, be eligible to receive retired pay, and:

- Retire from military service based on longevity, including Temporary Early Retirement Authority (TERA) retirees; or

- Retire due to disability with 20 or more qualifying years of service*; or

- Retire from National Guard or Reserve service with 20 or more qualifying years.

*For Veterans who retired due to disability with 20 or more qualifying years, CRDP is subject to an offset for the difference between retired pay based on disability and retired pay based on longevity.

**Housing Grants for Disabled Veterans:** Servicemembers and Veterans with certain service-connected disabilities may be entitled to a housing grant from VA to help build a new specially adapted house, to adapt a home they already own, or buy a house and modify it to meet their disability-related requirements. Eligible Veterans or Servicemembers may now receive up to three uses of the grant, with the total dollar amount of the grants not to exceed the maximum allowable. Housing grant amounts may be adjusted Oct. 1 every year based on a cost-of-construction index. These adjustments will increase the grant amounts or leave them unchanged; grant amounts will not decrease. Previous grant recipients who had received assistance of less than the current maximum allowable may be eligible for an additional grant usage. To obtain general information about the Specially Adapted Housing program, go to www.benefits.va.gov/homeloans/adaptedhousing.asp, or call the program's local office of jurisdiction at 1-877-827-3702.

**Specially Adapted Housing (SAH) Grant:** VA may approve a grant of not more than 50 percent of the cost of building, buying, or adapting existing homes or paying to reduce indebtedness on a currently owned home that is being adapted, up to a maximum of $73,768. In certain instances, the full grant amount may be applied toward remodeling costs. The SAH grant is available to certain Veterans and Servicemembers who are entitled to disability compensation due to the following:

1. Loss or loss of use of both lower extremities, which so affects the functions of balance or propulsion to preclude ambulating without the aid of braces, crutches, canes or a wheelchair.

2. Loss or loss of use of both upper extremities at or above the elbow.

3. Blindness in both eyes, having only light perception, plus loss or loss of use of one lower extremity.

4. Loss or loss of use of one lower extremity together with (a) residuals of organic disease or injury, or (b) the loss or loss of use of one upper extremity which so affects the functions of balance or propulsion as to preclude locomotion without the use of braces, canes, crutches or a wheelchair.

5. Severe burn injuries, which are defined as full thickness or subdermal burns that have resulted in contractures with limitation of motion of two or more extremities or of at least one extremity and the trunk.

6. The loss, or loss of use of one or more lower extremities due to service on or after September 11, 2001, which

so affects the functions of balance or propulsion as to preclude ambulating without the aid of braces, crutches, canes, or a wheelchair.

The property may be located outside the United States, in a country or political subdivision which allows individuals to have or acquire a beneficial property interest, and in which the Secretary of Veterans Affairs, in his or her discretion, has determined that it is reasonably practicable to provide assistance in acquiring specially adapted housing. For more information on SAH, visit www.benefits.va.gov/homeloans/adaptedhousing.asp or call the program's local office of jurisdiction at 1-877-827-3702.

**Special Home Adaption (SHA) Grant:** VA may approve a benefit amount up to a maximum of $14,754 for the cost of necessary adaptations to a Servicemember's or Veteran's residence or to help him/her acquire a residence already adapted with special features for his/her disability, to purchase and adapt a home, or for adaptations to a family member's home in which they will reside. To be eligible for this grant, Servicemembers and Veterans must be entitled to compensation for permanent and total service-connected disability due to one of the following:

1. Blindness in both eyes with 20/200 visual acuity or less.

2. Anatomical loss or loss of use of both hands.

3. Severe burn injuries (see above).

4. Certain severe respiratory injuries.

**Temporary Residence Adaptation (TRA):** Eligible Veterans and Servicemembers who are temporarily residing in a home owned by a family member may also receive a TRA grant to help the Veteran or Servicemember adapt the family member's home to meet his/her special needs. Those eligible for a $73,768 SAH grant would be permitted to use up to $32,384, and those eligible for a $14,754 SHA grant would be permitted to use up to $5,782. Under the Honoring America's Veterans and Caring for Camp Lejeune Families Act of 2012, TRA grant amounts do not count against SAH or

SHA grant maximum amounts, starting Aug. 6, 2013.

**Supplemental Financing:** Veterans and Servicemembers with available VA Home Loan guaranty entitlement may also obtain a guaranteed loan to supplement the grant to acquire a specially adapted home.

**Vocational Rehabilitation and Employment (VR&E):** VR&E provides services to eligible Servicemembers and Veterans with service-connected disabilities and an employment handicap, to help them prepare for, obtain, and maintain suitable employment. For Veterans and Servicemembers with service-connected disabilities so severe that they cannot immediately consider work, VR&E provides services to improve their ability to live as independently as possible. Additional information on VR&E benefits is available at www.benefits. va.gov/vocrehab.

**VR&E Eligibility for Veterans:** A Veteran must have a VA service-connected disability rating of at least 20 percent with an employment handicap or a rating of 10 percent with a serious employment handicap, and be discharged or released from military service under other than dishonorable conditions.

**VR&E Eligibility for Servicemembers:** Servicemembers are eligible to apply if they expect to receive an honorable discharge upon separation from active duty, obtain a rating of 20 percent or more from VA, obtain a proposed Disability Evaluation System (DES) rating of 20 percent or more from VA, or obtain a referral to a Physical Evaluation Board (PEB) through the Integrated Disability Evaluation System (IDES).

**VR&E Entitlement:** A vocational rehabilitation counselor (VRC) works with the Veteran to determine if an employment handicap exists. An employment handicap exists if a Veteran's service-connected disability impairs his/her ability to prepare for, obtain, or maintain suitable career employment. After an entitlement decision is made, the Veteran and VRC work together to develop an individualized rehabilitation plan. The individualized rehabilitation plan outlines the rehabilitation services to be provided.

**VR&E Services:** Based on their individualized needs, Veterans work with a VRC to select one of five tracks to employment. The five tracks to employment provide greater emphasis on exploring employment options early in the rehabilitation planning process, greater informed choice for the Veteran regarding occupational and employment options, faster access to employment for Veterans who have identifiable and transferable skills for direct placement into suitable employment, and an option for Veterans who are not able to work, but need assistance to lead a more independent life. If a program of training is selected, VA pays the cost of the approved training and services (except those coordinated through other providers) that are included in an individual's rehabilitation plan, including subsistence allowance.

**The Five Tracks to Employment are:**
- Reemployment with previous employer

- Rapid access to employment

- Self-employment

- Employment through long-term services

- Independent living services


**Length of a Rehabilitation Program**: The basic period of eligibility in which VR&E benefits may be used is 12 years from the later of the following: 1) A Veteran's date of separation from active military service, or 2) The date VA first notified a Veteran that he/she has a compensable service-connected disability. Depending on the length of program needed, Veterans may be provided up to 48 months of full-time services or the part-time equivalent. Rehabilitation plans that only provide services to improve independence in daily living are limited to 24 months. These limitations may be extended in certain circumstances.

**Employment Services**: VR&E establishes partnerships with federal, state, and private agencies that help facilitate direct placement of Veterans or Servicemembers into civilian careers. VR&E can assist with placement using the following resources:

**On the Job Training (OJT) Program**: Employers hire Veterans at an apprentice wage and VR&E supplements the salary up to the journeyman wage (up to the maximum allowable under OJT). As Veterans progress through training, employers begin to pay more of the salary until the Veterans reach journeyman level and the employers are paying the entire salary. VR&E will also pay for any necessary tools.

**Non-Paid Work Experience (NPWE):** The NPWE program provides eligible Veterans the opportunity to obtain training and practical job experience concurrently. This program is ideal for Veterans or Servicemembers who have a clearly established career goal, and who learn easily in a hands-on environment. This program is also well suited for Veterans who are having difficulties obtaining employment due to lack of work experience. The NPWE program may be established in a federal, state, or local (i.e. city, town, school district) government agency only. The employer may hire the Veteran at any point during the NPWE.

**Special Employer Incentive (SEI):** The SEI program is for eligible Veterans who face challenges in obtaining employment. Veterans approved to participate in the SEI program are hired by participating employers and employment is expected to continue following successful completion of the program. Employers may be provided this incentive to hire Veterans. If approved, the employer will receive reimbursement for up to 50 percent of the Veteran's salary during the SEI program, which can last up to six months.

**The Veterans Employment Center** (www.ebenefits.va.gov/ebenefits/jobs) is the Federal Government's single online source for connecting transitioning Servicemembers, Veterans, and military families with meaningful career opportunities with both public and private-sector employers.

**VetSuccess On Campus (VSOC):** The VSOC program is designed to assist Veterans as they make the transition to college life. Through VSOC, VR&E is strengthening partnerships with institutions of higher learning and creating opportunities to help Veterans achieve success by providing outreach and transition services to the general Veteran population during their transition from military to college life.

**Chapter 36 Education and Career Counseling:** VA's Education and Career Counseling Program (Title 38 U.S.C. Chapter 36) offers a great opportunity for transitioning Veterans, Servicemembers, and dependents to get personalized counseling and support to guide their career paths, ensure the most effective use of their VA benefits, and help them achieve their goals.

**VA Pension**: VA helps Veterans and their families cope with financial challenges by providing supplemental income through the Veterans Pension and Survivors Pension benefit programs. Payments are made to bring the Veteran's or Survivor's total income, including other retirement or Social Security income, to a level set by Congress. Unreimbursed medical expenses may reduce countable income for VA purposes.

**Veterans Pension**: Congress establishes the maximum annual Veterans Pension rates. Payments are reduced by the amount of countable income of the Veteran, spouse, and dependent children. When a Veteran without a spouse or a child is furnished nursing home or domiciliary care by VA, the pension is reduced to an amount not to exceed $90 per month after three calendar months of care. The reduction may be delayed if nursing-home care is being continued to provide the Veteran with rehabilitation services.

**Eligibility for Veterans Pension:** Generally, a Veteran must have at least 90 days of active duty service, with at least one day during a wartime period to qualify for a VA pension. Veterans who entered active duty after September 7, 1980, generally must have served at least 24 months or the full period for which called or ordered to active duty (with some exceptions), with at least one day during a wartime period. In addition to meeting minimum service requirements, low-income wartime Veterans may qualify for pension if they meet certain income and net worth limits set by law and are:

- Age 65 or older, OR

- Totally and permanently, OR

- A patient in a nursing home receiving skilled nursing care, OR

- Receiving Social Security Disability Insurance, OR

- Receiving Supplemental Security Income

Yearly family income must be less than the amount set by Congress to qualify for the Veterans Pension benefit. **Note:** Veterans may have to meet longer minimum periods of active duty if they entered active duty on or after Sept. 8, 1980, or, if they were officers who entered active duty on or after Oct. 16, 1981. The Veteran's discharge must have been under conditions other than dishonorable and the disability must be for reasons other than the Veteran's own willful misconduct.

**Aid and Attendance and Housebound Benefits (Special Monthly Pension):** Veterans and survivors who are eligible for a VA pension and require the aid and attendance of another person, or are housebound, may be eligible for a higher maximum pension rate. These benefits are paid in addition to monthly pension, and they are not paid without eligibility to pension. Since aid and attendance and housebound allowances increase the pension amount, people who are not eligible for a basic pension due to excessive income may be eligible for pension at these increased rates. A Veteran or surviving spouse may not receive aid and attendance benefits and housebound benefits at the same time.

**Education and Training:** Additional information can be found at www.benefits.va.gov/gibill or by calling 1-888-GI-BILL-1 (1-888-442-4551).

**Post-9/11 GI Bill®:** The Post-9/11 GI Bill is an education benefit program for Servicemembers and Veterans who served on active duty after Sept.10, 2001. Benefits are payable for training pursued on or after Aug. 1, 2009. No payments can be made under this program for training pursued before that date.

**Post-9/11 GI Bill Eligibility:** To be eligible, the Servicemember or Veteran must serve at least 90 aggregate days on active duty after Sept. 10, 2001, and remain on active duty or be honorably discharged. Active duty includes active service performed by National Guard members under title 32 U.S.C. for the purposes of organizing, administering, recruiting, instructing, or training the National Guard; or under section 502(f) for the purpose of responding to a national emergency. Veterans may also be eligible if they were honorably discharged from active duty for a service-connected disability after serving 30 continuous days after Sept. 10, 2001. Generally, Servicemembers or Veterans may receive up to 36 months of entitlement under the Post-9/11 GI Bill.

Eligibility for benefits expires 15 years from the last period of active duty of at least 90 consecutive days. If released for a service-connected disability after at least 30 days of continuous service, eligibility ends 15 years from when the member is released for the service-connected disability.

If, on Aug. 1, 2009, the Servicemember or Veteran is eligible for the Montgomery GI Bill; the Montgomery GI Bill – Selected Reserve; or the Reserve Educational Assistance Program, and qualifies for the Post-9/11 GI Bill, an irrevocable election must be made to receive benefits under the Post-9/11 GI Bill. In most instances, once the election to receive benefits under the Post-9/11 GI Bill is made, the individual will no longer be eligible to receive benefits under the relinquished program. Based on the length of active duty service, eligible participants are entitled to receive a percentage of the following:

- The cost of in-state tuition and fees at public institutions; the tuition and fees are capped at a national maximum rate for those attending private or foreign schools. Current rates can be found at www.benefits.va.gov/GIBILL/resources/benefits_resources/rate_tables.asp. Tuition and fees are paid to the institution on the student's behalf.

- Monthly housing allowance* based on the Department of Defense Basic Allowance for Housing (BAH) payable to a military E-5 with dependents, in the same ZIP code as the primary school (paid directly to the Veteran or eligible dependents),

- Yearly books and supplies stipend of up to $1,000 per year (paid directly to the Servicemember, Veteran, or eligible dependents), and

- A one-time payment of $500 paid to certain individuals relocating from highly rural areas.

*Housing allowance is not payable to individuals pursuing training at half time or less, to Servicemembers, or to spouses using transferred benefits of a Servicemember.

Approved training under the Post-9/11 GI Bill includes graduate and undergraduate degrees, vocational/technical training, on-the-job training, flight training, correspondence training, licensing and national testing programs, and tutorial assistance. Individuals serving an aggregate period of active duty after Sept. 10, 2001, can receive the following percentages of benefits described above based on length of service:

| Service Requirements - After 9/10/01, an individual must serve an aggregate of: | Payment Tiers Percentage |
|---|---|
| At least 36 months | 100% |
| At least 30 continuous days on active duty and discharged due to a service-connected disability | 100% |
| At least 30 months, but less than 36 months | 90% |
| At least 24 months, but less than 30 months | 80% |
| *At least 18 months, but less than 24 months | 70% |
| *At least 12 months, but less than 18 months | 60% |
| *At least 6 months, but less than 12 months | 50% |
| *At least 90 days, but less than 6 months | 40% |

*Excludes time in basic military training and/or skill training

**Yellow Ribbon G.I. Bill Education Enhancement Program**: The Yellow Ribbon Program allows institutions of higher learning (such as colleges, universities, and other degree-granting schools) in the United States to voluntarily enter into an agreement with VA to fund tuition and fees that exceed the amounts payable under the Post-9/11 GI Bill. The institution can contribute a specified dollar amount of those expenses, and VA will match the contribution, not to exceed 50 percent of the difference. To be eligible, the student must be a Veteran receiving benefits at the 100-percent benefit rate, a transfer-of-entitlement-eligible dependent child, or a transfer-of-entitlement-eligible spouse of a Veteran.

**Marine Gunnery Sergeant John David Fry Scholarship**: The Marine Gunnery Sergeant John David Fry Scholarship provides Post-9/11 GI Bill® benefits to the children and surviving spouses of Servicemembers who died in the line of duty after September 10, 2001. Eligible beneficiaries attending school may receive up to 36 months of benefits at the 100% level. NOTE: Fry Scholarship beneficiaries are not eligible for Yellow Ribbon Program benefits. The Fry

Scholarship includes:

- Full tuition and fees paid directly to the school for all public school in-state students. For those attending private or foreign schools, tuition and fees are capped at a statutory maximum amount per academic year.

- A monthly housing allowance

- A books and supplies stipend

**Marine Gunnery Sergeant John David Fry Scholarship Eligibility**: Children of active duty members of the Armed Forces who died in the line of duty after September 10, 2001, are eligible for this benefit. A child may begin an approved program of education before the age of 18. Eligibility ends on the child's 33rd birthday. A child's marital status has no effect on eligibility. Eligible children:

- Are entitled to 36 months of benefits at the 100-percent level

- Have 15 years to use the benefit beginning on their 18th birthday

- May use the benefit until their 33rd birthday

- Are not eligible for the Yellow Ribbon Program

Surviving spouses of active duty members of the Armed Forces who died in the line of duty after Sept.10, 2001, are eligible for this benefit. A surviving spouse's eligibility generally ends 15 years after the Servicemember's death. A spouse will lose eligibility to this benefit upon remarriage.

**Montgomery GI Bill Active Duty (MGIB-AD):** The MGIB-AD (Chapter 30) is an education benefit that provides up to 36 months of education benefits to eligible Veterans and Servicemembers for college degree and certificate programs, technical or vocational courses, flight training, apprenticeships or on-the-job training, high tech training, licensing and certification test, entrepreneurship training, certain entrance examinations, and correspondence courses. Remedial, deficiency, and refresher courses may be approved under certain circumstances. Benefits generally expire 10 years after discharge. Current payment rates are available at www.benefits.va.gov/gibill/.

A Veteran may be eligible for this benefit if he or she entered active duty after June 30, 1985, has an honorable discharge, did not decline MGIB in writing, and served three continuous years of active duty (or have an obligation to serve four years in the Selected Reserve after

27

active duty service). There are exceptions for disability, re-entering active duty, and upgraded discharges. All participants must have a high school diploma, equivalency certificate, or have completed 12 hours toward a college degree before applying for benefits.

**Home Loan Guaranty:** VA Home Loan guaranties are issued to help eligible Servicemembers, Veterans, Reservists, National Guard Members, and certain surviving spouses obtain homes, condominiums, and manufactured homes, and to refinance loans. Although it is preferable to apply electronically, it is possible to apply for a Certificate of Eligibility (COE) using VA Form 26-1880, *Request for Certificate of Eligibility.* In applying for a hard-copy COE from the VA Eligibility Center using VA Form 26-1880, it is typically necessary for the eligible Veteran to present a copy of his/her report of discharge or DD Form 214, *Certificate of Release or Discharge from Active Duty,* or other adequate substitute evidence to VA. An eligible active duty Servicemember should obtain and submit a statement of service signed by an appropriate military official to the VA Eligibility Center.

| Veterans living in: | Please send completed applications to: |
|---|---|
| Georgia, North Carolina, South Carolina, Tennessee | Department of Veterans Affairs Atlanta Regional Loan Center P.O. Box 100023 Decatur, GA  30031-7023 |
| Connecticut, Delaware, Indiana, Maine, Massachusetts, Michigan, New Hampshire,  New Jersey, New York, Ohio, Pennsylvania, Rhode Island,  Vermont | Department of Veterans Affairs Cleveland Regional Loan Center 1240 East Ninth Street Cleveland, OH  44199 |
| Alaska, Colorado, Idaho, Montana, Oregon, Utah, Washington, Wyoming, | Department of Veterans Affairs Denver Regional Loan Center Box 25126 Denver, CO  80225 |
| Hawaii, Guam, American Samoa, Commonwealth of the Northern Marianas | Department of Veterans Affairs VA Regional Office Loan Guaranty Division (26) 459 Patterson Road Honolulu, HI  96819 |

| | |
|---|---|
| Arkansas, Louisiana, Oklahoma, Texas | Department of Veterans Affairs<br>Houston Regional Loan Center<br>6900 Almeda Road<br>Houston, TX 77030-4200 |
| Arizona, California, New Mexico, Nevada | Department of Veterans Affairs<br>Phoenix Regional Loan Center<br>3333 North Central Avenue<br>Phoenix, AZ 85012-2402 |
| District of Columbia, Kentucky, Maryland, Virginia, West Virginia | Department of Veterans Affairs<br>Roanoke Regional Loan Center<br>210 Franklin Road, S.W.<br>Roanoke, VA 24011 |
| Illinois, Iowa, Kansas, Minnesota, Missouri, Nebraska, North Dakota, South Dakota, Wisconsin | Department of Veterans Affairs<br>St. Paul Regional Loan Center<br>1 Federal Drive, Ft. Snelling<br>St. Paul, MN 55111-4050 |
| Alabama, Florida, Mississippi, Puerto Rico, U.S. Virgin Islands | Department of Veterans Affairs<br>St. Petersburg Regional Loan Center<br>P.O. Box 1437<br>St. Petersburg, FL 33731 |

The completed VA Form 26-1880 and any associated documentation should be mailed to the Regional Loan Center of jurisdiction as listed in the table above. For general program information or to obtain VA loan guaranty forms, visit www.benefits.va.gov/homeloans/ or call 1-877-827-3702 to reach the home loan program's local office of jurisdiction.

Please note that while VA's electronic applications can often establish eligibility and issue an online COE in a matter of seconds, the system can only process cases for which VA has sufficient data in its records. Therefore, certain applicants will not be able to establish eligibility online and additional information might be requested prior to the issuance of a COE. If a COE cannot be issued immediately, users have the option of submitting an electronic application.

**Home Loan Guaranty Uses:** A VA loan guaranty helps protect lenders from loss if the borrower fails to repay the loan. It can be used to obtain a loan to:
1. Buy or build a home.

29

2.  Buy a residential condominium unit.
3.  Repair, alter, or improve a residence owned by the Veteran and occupied as a home.
4.  Refinance an existing home loan.
5.  Buy a manufactured home and/or lot.
6.  Install a solar heating or cooling system or other energy-efficient improvements.

**Home Loan Guaranty Eligibility:** In addition to the periods of eligibility and conditions of service requirements, applicants must have a good credit rating, sufficient income, a valid COE, and agree to live in the property in order to be approved by a lender for a VA home loan. Lenders can apply for a COE online through the Veterans Information Portal (https://vip.vba.va.gov/portal/VBAH/Home). Active duty Servicemembers and Veterans can also apply online at www.ebenefits.va.gov.

**Home Loan Guaranty Periods of Eligibility and Service Requirements**
World War II: (1) Active duty service after Sept.15, 1940, and prior to July 26, 1947; (2) Discharge under other than dishonorable conditions; and (3) At least 90 days total service unless discharged early for a service-connected disability.

Post-World War II period: (1) Active duty service after July 25, 1947, and prior to June 27, 1950; (2) Discharge under other than dishonorable conditions; and (3) 181 days continuous active duty service unless discharged early for a service-connected disability.

**Korean War:** (1) Active duty after June 26, 1950, and prior to Feb. 1, 1955; (2) Discharge under other than dishonorable conditions; and (3) At least 90 days total service, unless discharged early for a service-connected disability.

**Post-Korean War period:** (1) Active duty after Jan. 31, 1955, and prior to Aug. 5, 1964; (2) Discharge under other than dishonorable conditions; (3) 181 days continuous service, unless discharged early for a service-connected disability.
**Vietnam War:** (1) Active duty after Aug. 4, 1964, and prior to May 8, 1975; (2) Discharge under other than dishonorable conditions; and (3) 90 days total service, unless discharged early for a service-connected disability. For Veterans who served in the Republic of

Vietnam, the beginning date is Feb. 28, 1961.

**Post-Vietnam period:** (1) Active duty after May 7, 1975, and prior to Aug. 2, 1990; (2) Active duty for 181 continuous days, all of which occurred after May 7, 1975; and (3) Discharge under conditions other than dishonorable or early discharge for service-connected disability. 24-Month Rule:

If service was between Sept. 8, 1980, (Oct. 16, 1981, for officers) and Aug. 1, 1990, Veterans must generally complete 24 months of continuous active duty service or the full period (at least 181 days) for which they were called or ordered to active duty, and be discharged under conditions other than dishonorable. Exceptions are allowed if the Veteran completed at least 181 days of active duty service but was discharged earlier than 24 months for (1) hardship, (2) the convenience of the government, (3) reduction-in-force, (4) certain medical conditions, or (5) service-connected disability.

**Gulf War:** Veterans of the Gulf War era – Aug. 2, 1990, to a date to be determined – must generally complete 24 months of continuous active duty service or the full period (at least 90 days) for which they were called to active duty, and be discharged under other than dishonorable conditions. Exceptions are allowed if the Veteran completed at least 90 days of active duty but was discharged earlier than 24 months for (1) hardship, (2) the convenience of the government, (3) reduction-in-force, (4) certain medical conditions, or (5) service-connected disability.

**Active Duty Personnel:** Until the Gulf War era is ended, persons on active duty are eligible after serving 90 continuous days.

**Reservists and National Guard members (activated):** Eligible if they were (1) Activated after Aug. 1, 1990, and completed the full period for which they were called to active duty, (2) Served at least 90 days, and (3) Discharged under other than dishonorable conditions.

**Reserves and Guard (not activated):** Members of the Reserves and National Guard who are not otherwise eligible for loan guaranty benefits are eligible upon completing 6 years of service in the Reserves or Guard (unless released earlier due to a service-connected disability). The applicant must have received an honorable (a general or under honorable conditions is not qualifying) discharge from such service unless he/she is either in an inactive status awaiting final discharge, or still serving in the Reserves or Guard.

**Surviving Spouses:** Some spouses of Veterans may have home loan eligibility: the unmarried surviving spouse of a Veteran who died as a result of service or service-connected causes, the surviving spouse of a Veteran who dies on active duty or from service-connected causes and who remarries on or after attaining age 57 and on or after Dec. 16, 2003; the spouse of an active duty member who is listed as missing in action (MIA) or a prisoner of war (POW) for at least 90 days.

Eligibility under the MIA/POW provision is limited to one-time use only. Surviving spouses of Veterans who died from nonservice-connected causes may also be eligible if any of the following conditions are met: the Veteran was rated totally service-connected disabled for 10 years or more immediately preceding death, or was rated totally disabled for not less than five years from date of discharge or release from active duty to date of death, or was a former prisoner of war who died after Sept. 30, 1999, and was rated totally service-connected disabled for not less than one year immediately preceding death.

**Home Loan Guaranty Loan Limits**: VA does not make loans to Veterans and Servicemembers; VA guarantees loans made by private-sector lenders. The guaranty is what VA could pay a lender should the loan go to foreclosure. VA does not set a cap on how much an individual can borrow to finance a home.

However, there are limits on the amount of liability VA can assume, which usually affects the amount of money an institution will lend. The loan limits are the amount a qualified Veteran with full entitlement may be able to borrow without making a downpayment. These loan limits vary by county, since the value of a house depends in part on its location. For a list of loan limits based on the corresponding county please visit: www.benefits.va.gov/homeloans/purchaseco_loan_limits.asp.

It is important to note that VA does not impose a maximum loan amount that a Veteran may borrow to purchase a home; instead, the law directs the maximum amount that VA may guarantee on a home loan. Because most VA loans are pooled in mortgage securities that require a 25-percent guaranty, the effective no-downpayment loan limit on VA loans is typically four times VA's maximum guaranty amount. Loans for more than this effective limit generally require down payments. VA's effective no-downpayment loan limits are established annually, and vary depending on the size of the loan and the location of the property.

**Other Types of Loans**: An eligible borrower can use a VA-guaranteed Interest Rate Reduction Refinancing Loan to refinance an existing VA loan and lower the interest rate and payment. Typically, no credit underwriting is required for this type of loan. The loan may include the entire outstanding balance of the prior loan, the costs of energy-efficient improvements, and closing costs, including up to two discount points.

An eligible borrower who wishes to obtain a VA-guaranteed loan to purchase a manufactured home or lot can borrow up to 95 percent of the home's purchase price. The amount VA will guarantee on a manufactured home loan is 40 percent of the loan amount or the Veteran's available entitlement, up to a maximum amount of $20,000. These provisions apply only to a manufactured home that will not be placed on a permanent foundation.

**Home Loan Guaranty Appraisals**: A home appraisal by a VA-assigned fee appraiser is required for purchase and certain refinance loans guaranteed by VA. A lender can request a VA appraisal through VA systems. The Veteran borrower typically pays for the appraisal upon completion, according to a fee schedule approved by VA. The VA appraisal estimates the value of the property. An appraisal is not an inspection and does not guarantee the house is free of defects. VA guarantees the loan, not the condition of the property.

A thorough inspection of the property by a reputable inspection firm may help minimize any problems that could arise after loan closing. In an existing home, particular attention should be given to plumbing, heating, electrical, roofing, and structural components. In addition, VA strongly recommends testing for radon, a known carcinogen.

**Home Loan Guaranty Closing Costs**: For purchase home loans, payment in cash is required on all closing costs, including title search and recording fees, hazard insurance premiums, and prepaid taxes. For refinancing loans, all such costs may be included in the loan, as long as the total loan does not exceed the reasonable value of the property. Interest rate reduction loans may include closing costs, including a maximum of two discount points.

**Home Loan Guaranty Funding Fees**: The funding fee is a percentage of the loan amount collected in order to offset future anticipated costs associated with the loan. A funding fee must be paid to VA unless the Veteran is, by law, exempt from such a fee. Currently, exemptions from the funding fee are provided for Veterans and Servicemembers receiving VA disability compensation, those who are rated by VA as eligible to receive compensation as a result of pre-discharge disability examination and rating, and those who would be in receipt of compensation, but who were recalled to active duty or reenlisted and are receiving active-duty pay in lieu of compensation. Additionally, unmarried surviving spouses in receipt of dependency and indemnity compensation may be exempt.

The table on page 35 provides current VA funding fee rates. The fee may be paid in cash or included in the loan. For all types of loans, the loan amount may include the VA funding fee and up to $6,000 of energy-efficient improvements.

However, no other fees (including fees for the VA appraisal, credit report, loan processing, title search, title insurance, recording fees, transfer taxes, survey charges, or hazard insurance), charges, or discount points may be included in loans for purchase or construction. For refinancing loans, most closing costs may be included in the loan amount.

| 2015 VA Funding Fee Rates | | |
|---|---|---|
| Loan Category | Active Duty and Veterans | Reserve and National Guard |
| Loans for purchase or construction with down-payments of less than 5 percent, refinancing, and home improvement | 2.15 percent | 2.40 percent |
| Loans for purchase or construction with down-payments of at least 5 percent but less than 10 percent | 1.50 percent | 1.75 percent |
| Loans for purchase or construction with down-payments of 10 percent or more | 1.25 percent | 1.50 percent |
| Loans for manufactured homes | 1 percent | 1 percent |
| Interest rate reduction refinancing loans | .50 percent | .50 percent |
| Assumption of a VA- guaranteed loan | .50 percent | .50 percent |
| Second or subsequent use of entitlement with no downpayment | 3.3 percent | 3.3 percent |

**Home Loan Guaranty Required Occupancy**: To qualify for a VA home loan, a Veteran or the spouse of an active-duty Service-member must certify that he or she intends to occupy the home. A dependent child of an active-duty Servicemember also satisfies the occupancy requirement. When refinancing a VA-guaranteed loan solely to reduce the interest rate, a Veteran only needs to certify prior occupancy.

**Home Loan Guaranty Financing, Interest Rates, and Terms**:
Veterans obtain VA-guaranteed loans through the usual lending
institutions including banks, credit unions, and mortgage brokers.
VA-guaranteed loans can have either a fixed interest rate or an
adjustable rate where the interest rate may adjust up to one percent
annually and up to five percent over the life of the loan. VA does not
set the interest rate. Interest rates are negotiable between the lender
and borrower on all loan types.

Veterans may also choose a different type of adjustable rate mortgage called a hybrid ARM, where the initial interest rate remains
fixed for 3-10 years. If the rate remains fixed for less than five years,
the rate adjustment cannot be more than one percent annually and
five percent over the life of the loan. For a hybrid ARM with an initial
fixed period of five years or more, the initial adjustment may be up to
two percent.

The Secretary has the authority to determine annual adjustments
thereafter. Currently, annual adjustments may be up to two percentage points and six percent over the life of the loan.
If the lender charges discount points on the loan, the Veteran may
negotiate with the seller as to who will pay points or if they will be
split between buyer and seller. Points paid by the Veteran may not
be included in the loan (with the exception that up to two points may
be included in interest rate reduction refinancing loans). The term of
the loan may be for as long as 30 years and 32 days.

**Home Loan Guaranty Loan Assumption Requirements and Li-
ability**: VA loans made on or after March 1, 1988, are not assumable
without the prior approval of VA or its authorized agent (usually the
lender collecting the monthly payments). To approve the assumption,
the lender must ensure that the purchaser is a satisfactory credit
risk and will assume all of the Veteran's liabilities on the loan. If approved, the purchaser will have to pay a funding fee that the lender
sends to VA, and the Veteran will be released from liability to the
Federal Government. (A VA-guaranteed loan may be assumed by
Veterans, active duty personnel, and non-Veterans alike.)

Loans made prior to March 1, 1988, are generally freely assumable,
but Veterans should still request the lender's approval in order to be
released of liability. Veterans whose loans were closed after Dec. 31,
1989, usually have no liability to the government following a foreclo-

sure, except in cases involving fraud, misrepresentation, or bad faith, such as allowing an unapproved assumption. However, for the entitlement to be restored, any loss suffered by VA must be paid in full.

A release of liability does not mean that a Veteran's guaranty entitlement is restored. That occurs only if the borrower is an eligible Veteran who agrees to substitute his or her entitlement for that of the seller. If a Veteran allows assumption of a loan without prior approval, then the lender may demand immediate and full payment of the loan, and the Veteran may be liable if the loan is foreclosed and VA has to pay a claim under the loan guaranty.

**VA Assistance to Veterans in Default**: When a VA-guaranteed home loan becomes delinquent, VA may provide supplemental servicing assistance to help cure the default. The servicer has the primary responsibility of servicing the loan to resolve the default, and VA urges all Veterans who are encountering problems making their mortgage payments to speak with their servicers as soon as possible to explore options to avoid foreclosure. Contrary to popular opinion, servicers do not want to foreclose because foreclosure costs money. Depending on a Veteran's specific situation, servicers may offer any of the following options to avoid foreclosure:

- Repayment Plan – The borrower makes a regular installment each month plus part of the missed installments.

- Special Forbearance – The servicer agrees not to initiate foreclosure to allow time for borrowers to repay the missed installments or agrees to place a hold or postpone foreclosure proceedings. An example of when this option might be offered is when a borrower is waiting for a tax refund.

- Loan Modification – Provides the borrower a fresh start by adding the delinquency to the loan balance and establishing a new payment schedule.

- Short Sale – When the servicer agrees to allow a borrower to sell his/her home for a lesser amount than what is currently required to pay off the loan.

- Deed-in-Lieu of Foreclosure – The borrower voluntarily agrees to deed the property to the servicer instead of going through a lengthy foreclosure process.

In cases where the servicer is unable to help the Veteran borrower, VA has loan technicians at its eight RLCs and in Hawaii, who are available to take an active role in interceding with the mortgage servicer. Veterans with VA-guaranteed home loans can call 1-877-827-3702 to discuss potential ways to help save the loan.

Veterans who believe they may be facing homelessness as a result of losing their home can call 1-877-4AIDVET (877-424-3838) or go to www.va.gov/HOMELESS/index.asp to receive assistance in preventing homelessness.

**Servicemembers Civil Relief Act (SCRA) and Home Loan Guaranties**: Veteran borrowers may be able to request relief pursuant to SCRA. In order to qualify for certain protections available under the Act, their obligation must have originated prior to their current period of active military service. SCRA may provide a lower interest rate during military service and for up to one year after service ends, provide forbearance, or prevent foreclosure or eviction up to nine months from period of military service.

**Assistance to Veterans with Non-VA-Guaranteed Home Loans in Default**: VA advises Veterans or Servicemembers who are having difficulty making payments on a non-VA-guaranteed loan to contact their servicer as quickly as possible to explore options to avoid foreclosure. Although for non-VA loans, VA does not have authority to directly intervene on the borrower's behalf, VA's network of loan technicians at eight RLCs and an office in Hawaii can offer advice and guidance on how to potentially avoid foreclosure. Veterans or Servicemembers with non-VA loans may call 1-877-827-3702 to speak with a VA loan technician, or visit www.benefits.va.gov/homeloans for more information on avoiding foreclosure.

If VA is not able to help a Veteran borrower retain his/her home (whether a VA-guaranteed loan or not), the Department of Housing and Urban Development (HUD) offers assistance to homeowners by sponsoring local housing counseling agencies. To find an approved agency in your area, search online at www.hud.gov/offices/hsg/sfh/hcc/hcs.cfm or call HUD's interactive voice system at 1-800-569-4287.

**VA Acquired Property Sales**: VA acquires properties as a result of foreclosures of VA-guaranteed and VA-owned loans. A private contractor currently markets the acquired properties through listing agents using local Multiple Listing Services. A listing of "VA Properties for Sale" may be found at http://listings.vrmco.com/. Contact a real estate agent for information on purchasing a VA-acquired property.

**Loans for Native American Veterans:** Eligible Native American Veterans can obtain a loan from VA to purchase, construct, or improve a home on federal Trust Land, or to reduce the interest rate on such a VA loan. Native American Direct Loans (NADLs) are only available if a memorandum of understanding exists between the tribal organization and VA. Veterans who are not Native American, but who are married to Native American non-Veterans, may be eligible for a direct loan under this program.

To be eligible for such a loan, the qualified non-Native American Veteran and the Native American spouse must reside on federal Trust Land, both the Veteran and spouse must have a meaningful interest in the dwelling or lot, and the tribal authority that has jurisdiction over the Trust Land must recognize the non-Native American Veteran as subject to its authority. More information about the NADL program can be found at www.benefits.va.gov/homeloans/nadl.asp.

**VA Life Insurance**: VA's life insurance benefits include Servicemembers' Group Life Insurance, Veterans' Group Life Insurance, Family Servicemembers' Group Life Insurance, Servicemembers' Group Life Insurance Traumatic Injury Protection, Service-Disabled Veterans' Life Insurance, and Veterans' Mortgage Life Insurance. These programs are described below. Complete details are also available at www.benefits.va.gov/insurance; by writing to Department of Veterans Affairs, Insurance Center, PO Box 42954, Philadelphia, PA 19101; or by calling VA's Insurance Center toll-free at 1-800-669-8477. Specialists at the Insurance Center are available from 8:30 a.m. and 6 p.m., Eastern Time, to discuss premium payments, insurance dividends, address changes, policy loans, naming beneficiaries, reporting the death of the insured, and other insurance issues.

For information about Servicemembers' Group Life Insurance, Veterans' Group Life Insurance, Servicemembers' Group Life Insurance Traumatic Injury Protection, or Family Servicemembers' Group Life

Insurance, visit www.benefits.va.gov/insurance/ or call the Office of Servicemembers' Group Life Insurance directly at 1-800-419-1473.

**Servicemembers' Group Life Insurance (SGLI):** The following are automatically insured for $400,000 under SGLI:

1. Active duty members of the Army, Navy, Air Force, Marines, and Coast Guard.

2. Commissioned members of the National Oceanic and Atmospheric Administration (NOAA) and the Public Health Service (PHS).

3. Cadets or midshipmen of the U.S. military academies.

4. Members, cadets and midshipmen of the ROTC while engaged in authorized training and practice cruises.

5. Members of the Ready Reserves/National Guard who are scheduled to perform at least 12 periods of inactive training per year.

6. Members who volunteer for a mobilization category in the Individual Ready Reserve.

Individuals may elect in writing to be covered for a lesser amount or to decline coverage. SGLI coverage is available in $50,000 increments up to the maximum of $400,000. Full-time Servicemembers on active duty are covered 24/7, 365 days of the year. Coverage is in effect during the period of active duty or inactive duty training and for 120 days following separation or release from duty.

Reservists and National Guard members who have been assigned to a unit in which they are scheduled to perform at least 12 periods of inactive duty that is creditable for retirement purposes are also covered 24/7, 365 days of the year and for 120 days following separation or release from duty. Part-time coverage is provided for Reservists or National Guard members who do not qualify for the full-time coverage described above.

Part-time coverage generally applies to Reservists/National Guard members who drill only a few days in a year. These individuals are covered only while on active duty or active duty for training, or traveling to and from such duty. Members covered part-time do not receive

120 days of free coverage after separation unless they incur or aggravate a disability during a period of duty.

**SGLI Traumatic Injury Protection (TSGLI)**: TSGLI provides for payment to traumatically injured Servicemembers who have suffered certain physical losses. The TSGLI benefit ranges from $25,000 to $100,000, depending on the loss. TSGLI helps Servicemembers by allowing their families to be with them during their recovery or by helping with other expenses incurred during their recovery period.

TSGLI is attached to SGLI. An additional $1.00 is added to the Servicemember's SGLI premium to cover TSGLI. After Dec. 1, 2005, all Servicemembers who are covered by SGLI are automatically also covered by TSGLI. TSGLI cannot be declined unless the Servicemember also declines basic SGLI. TSGLI claims are adjudicated by the individual military branches of service. Retroactive TSGLI coverage is available for Servicemembers who suffered a traumatic injury between Oct. 7, 2001, and Nov. 30, 2005, that resulted in a qualifying loss, regardless of where the injury occurred. TSGLI coverage is payable to these Servicemembers regardless of whether they had SGLI coverage in force at the time of their injury.

For more information and branch of service contact information, visit http://benefits.va.gov/insurance/tsgli.asp, or call 1-800-237-1336 (Army); 1-866-827-5672, option2 (Navy); 1-877-216-0825 (Marine Corps); 1-800-433-0048 (Active Duty Air Force); 1-800-525-0102 (Air Force Reserves); 1-240-612-9173 (Air National Guard); 1-202-795-6647 (Coast Guard); 1-301-427-3280 (PHS); or 1-301-713-3444 (NOAA).

**Family Servicemembers' Group Life Insurance (FSGLI) Coverage**: FSGLI coverage consists of spousal and dependent child coverage. FSGLI provides up to $100,000 of life insurance coverage for spouses of Servicemembers with full-time SGLI coverage, not to exceed the amount of SGLI the member has in force. Coverage for spouses who are not in the military is automatic. For spouses who are in the military and were married on or after Jan. 2, 2013, coverage is not automatic. The member can apply for spousal coverage, but the spouse must meet good health requirements. Premiums for spouse coverage are based on the age of the spouse and the amount of FSGLI coverage. FSGLI is a Servicemembers' benefit; the member pays the premium and is the only person allowed to be the beneficiary of the coverage. FSGLI spousal coverage ends 120 days after any of the following events: 1) the Servicemember elects in writing to terminate coverage on the spouse; 2) the Servicemember elects to terminate his or her own SGLI coverage; 3) the Service-member dies; 4) the Servicemember separates from service; or 5) the Servicemember is divorced from the spouse. The insured spouse may convert his/her FSGLI coverage to a permanent policy offered by participating private insurers within 120 days of the date of any of the termination events noted above. FSGLI dependent coverage of $10,000 is also automatically provided for dependent children of Servicemembers insured under SGLI, with no premium required.

**Veterans' Group Life Insurance (VGLI)**: Following separation from service, SGLI may be converted to VGLI, which provides lifetime renewable term coverage to:

1.   Veterans who had full-time SGLI coverage upon separation from active duty or the Reserves.

2.   Members of the Ready Reserves/National Guard with part-time SGLI coverage who incur a disability or aggravate a pre-existing disability during a period of active duty or a period of inactive duty for less than 31 days that renders them uninsurable at stan-dard premium rates.

3.   Members of the Individual Ready Reserve (IRR) and Inactive National Guard (ING).

4.   Members placed on the Temporary Disability Retirement List (TDRL)

Servicemembers must apply for VGLI within one year and 120 days from separation. Servicemembers discharged on or after November 1, 2012, who apply for VGLI within 240 days of separation from ser-vice do not need to submit evidence of good health, while Service-members who apply after the 240-day period must submit evidence of insurability. The initial VGLI coverage available is equal to the amount of SGLI coverage at the time of separation from service. Effective April 11, 2011, VGLI insureds who are under age 60 and have less than $400,000 in coverage can purchase up to $25,000 of additional coverage on each five-year anniversary of their coverage, up to the maximum $400,000. No medical underwriting is required for the additional coverage.

**SGLI Disability Extension**: Servicemembers who are totally disabled at the time of separation (unable to work or have certain statutory conditions), can apply for the SGLI Disability Extension, which provides free coverage for up to two years from the date of separation. To apply, Servicemembers must complete and return SGLV 8715, the SGLI Disability Extension Application. Those covered under the SGLI Disability Extension are automatically converted to VGLI at the end of their extension period, subject to the payment of premiums. VGLI is convertible at any time to a permanent plan policy with any participating commercial insurance company.

**Accelerated Death Benefits**: Like many private life insurance companies, the SGLI, FSGLI, and VGLI programs offer an accelerated benefits option to terminally ill insured members. An insured member is considered to be terminally ill if he/she has a written medical prognosis of nine months or less to live. All terminally ill members are eligible to receive up to 50 percent of their SGLI or VGLI coverage, and terminally ill spouses can receive up to 50 percent of their FSGLI, in a lump sum. Payment of an accelerated benefit reduces the amount payable to the beneficiaries at the time of the insured's death. To apply, an insured member must submit SGLV 8284, Servicemember/Veteran Accelerated Benefit Option Form, available at www.benefits.va.gov/INSURANCE/forms/SGLV_8284.pdf. Spouses must complete SGLV 8284A, Servicemember Family Coverage Accelerated Benefits Option Form, available at www.benefits.va.gov/insurance/forms/SGLV_8284A.pdf.

**Service-Disabled Veterans Insurance (S-DVI)**: Veterans who separated from service on or after Apr. 25, 1951, under other than dishonorable conditions who have service-connected disabilities (even zero percent), but are otherwise in good health, may apply to VA for up to $10,000 in life insurance coverage under the S-DVI program. Applications must be submitted within two years from the date of being notified of the approval of a new service-connected disability by VA. Veterans who are totally disabled may apply for a waiver of premiums. If approved for a waiver of premiums, the Veteran can apply for additional supplemental insurance coverage of up to $30,000. However, premiums cannot be waived on the additional supplemental insurance. To be eligible for this type of supplemental insurance, Veterans must meet all of the following three requirements:

1. Be under age 65.

2. Be eligible for a waiver of premiums due to total disability.

3. Apply for additional insurance within one year from the date of notification of waiver approval on the basic S-DVI policy.

**Veterans' Mortgage Life Insurance (VMLI)**: VMLI is mortgage protection insurance available to severely disabled Veterans who have been approved by VA for a Specially Adapted Housing (SAH) Grant. Maximum coverage is the smaller of the existing mortgage balance or $200,000, and is payable only to the mortgage company. Protection is issued automatically following SAH approval, provided the Veteran submits mortgage information required to establish a premium and does not decline coverage. Coverage automatically terminates when the mortgage is paid off. If a mortgage is disposed of through sale of the property, VMLI may be obtained on the mortgage of another home.

**Other Insurance Information**: The following information applies only to policies issued to World War II, Korean-era, and Vietnam-era Veterans and any Service-Disabled Veterans' Insurance policies. Policies in this group are prefixed by the letters K, V, RS, W, J, JR, JS, or RH.

**Insurance Dividends Issued Annually**: World War II and Korean-era Veterans with active policies beginning with the letters V, RS, W, J, JR, JS, or K earn tax-free dividends annually on the policy anniversary date. Policies prefixed by RH do not earn dividends. Policyholders do not need to apply for dividends, but may select from among the following dividend options:
1. Cash: The dividend is paid directly to the insured by direct deposit to a bank account or by check.

2. Paid-Up Additional Insurance: The dividend is used to purchase additional insurance coverage.

3. Credit or Deposit: The dividend is held in an account for the policyholder with interest. Withdrawals from the account can be made at any time. The interest rate may be adjusted.

4. Net Premium Billing Options: These options use the dividend to pay the annual policy premium. If the dividend exceeds the pre-

mium, the policyholder has options to choose how the remainder is used. If the dividend is not enough to pay an annual premium, the policyholder is billed the balance.

5. Other Dividend Options: Dividends can also be used to repay a loan or pay premiums in advance.

**Reinstating Lapsed Insurance**: Lapsed term policies may be reinstated within 5 years from the date of lapse. A 5 year term policy that is not lapsed at the end of the term is automatically renewed for an additional 5 years. Lapsed permanent plans may be reinstated within certain time limits and with certain health requirements. Reinstated permanent plan policies require repayment of all back premiums, plus interest.

**Converting Term Policies**: Term policies are renewed automatically every 5 years, with premiums increasing at each renewal. Premiums do not increase after age 70. Term policies may be converted to permanent plans, which have fixed premiums for life and earn cash and loan values.

**Dividends on Capped Term Policies**: Effective September 2000, VA provides either a cash dividend or paid-up insurance on term policies whose premiums have been capped. Veterans with National Service Life Insurance (NSLI) term insurance that have renewed at age 71 or older and who stop paying premiums on their policies will be given a "termination dividend". This dividend can either be received as a cash payment or used to purchase a reduced amount of paid-up insurance, which insures the Veteran for life with no premium payments required. The amount of the reduced paid-up insurance remains level. This does not apply to S-DVI (RH) policies.

**Borrowing on Policies**: Policyholders with permanent plan policies may borrow up to 94 percent of the cash surrender value of their insurance after the insurance is in force for 1 year or more. Interest is compounded annually. The loan interest rate is variable and may be obtained by calling toll-free 1-800-669-8477.

**Reserve and National Guard Re-employment Rights**: A person who left a civilian job to enter active duty in the Armed Forces is entitled to return to the job after discharge or release from active duty if they:

1. Gave advance notice of military service to the employer.

2. Did not exceed 5 years cumulative absence from the civilian job (with some exceptions).

3. Submitted a timely application for re-employment.

4. Did not receive a dishonorable or other punitive discharge.

The law calls for a returning Veteran to be placed in the job as if he/she had never left, including benefits based on seniority such as pensions, pay increases, and promotions. The law also prohibits discrimination in hiring, promotion, or other advantages of employment on the basis of military service. Veterans seeking re-employment should apply, verbally or in writing, to the company's hiring official and keep a record of their application. If problems arise, contact the Department of Labor's Veterans' Employment and Training Service (VETS) in the state of the employer. Federal employees not properly re-employed may appeal directly to the Merit Systems Protection Board. Non-federal employees may file complaints in U.S. District Court. For additional information, visit www.dol.gov/vets/programs/userra/main.htm.

## Special Groups of Veterans

**Veterans and Survivors Needing Fiduciary Services**: The fiduciary program provides oversight of VA's most vulnerable beneficiaries who are unable to manage their VA benefits because of injury, disease, the infirmities of advanced age, or being under 18 years of age. VA appoints fiduciaries who manage VA benefits for these beneficiaries and conducts oversight of VA-appointed fiduciaries to ensure that they are meeting the needs of the beneficiaries they serve.

VA closely monitors fiduciaries for compliance with program responsibilities to ensure that VA benefits are being used for the purpose of meeting the needs, security, and comfort of beneficiaries and their dependents. In deciding who should act as fiduciary for a beneficiary, VA will always select the most effective and least restrictive fiduciary arrangement. For more information about VA's fiduciary program, please visit our website at http://benefits.va.gov/fiduciary/index.asp.

**Homeless Veterans**: VA's homeless programs constitute the largest integrated network of homeless assistance programs in the country, offering a wide array of services to help Veterans recover from homelessness and live as self-sufficiently and independently as possible. For more information on VA homeless programs and services, Veterans currently enrolled in VA health care can speak with their VA mental health or health care provider. Other Veterans and interested parties can find a complete list of VA health care facilities at www.va.gov, or they can call VA's general information hotline at 1-800-827-1000. If assistance is needed when contacting a VA facility, ask to speak to the Health Care for Homeless Veterans Program or the Mental Health service manager. Information is also available at www.va.gov/homeless.

**VA Health Care for Homeless Veterans (HCHV) Program:** The HCHV Program provides a gateway to VA and community supportive services for eligible Veterans. Through the HCHV Program, Veterans are provided with case management and residential treatment in the community. The program also conducts outreach to homeless Veterans who are not likely to come to VA facilities on their own.

**Homeless Veterans Supported Employment Program (HVSEP):** HVSEP provides vocational assistance, job development and placement, and ongoing employment supports designed to improve employment outcomes among homeless Veterans. HVSEP is coordinated between VA's Compensated Work Therapy Program and the continuum of Homeless Veterans Programs for the purpose of providing community-based vocational and employment services. For more information, please visit: www.va.gov/homeless/employment_programs.asp.

**VA's Homeless Providers Grant and Per Diem Program:** The program provides funds to non-profit community agencies providing transitional housing for up to 24 months and/or offering services to homeless Veterans, such as case management, education, crisis intervention, counseling, and services targeted towards specialized populations including homeless women Veterans. The goal of the program is to help homeless Veterans achieve residential stability, increase their skill levels and/or income, and obtain greater self-determination. For more information, please visit: www.va.gov/homeless/gpd.asp.

**Housing and Urban Development-Veterans Affairs Supportive Housing (HUD-VASH) Program:** The HUD-VASH Program provides permanent housing and case management for eligible homeless Veterans who need community-based support to keep stable housing. This program allows eligible Veterans to live in Veteran-selected housing units with a "Housing Choice" voucher. These vouchers are portable to support the Veteran's choice of housing in communities served by their VA medical facility where case management services can be provided. For more information, please visit: www.va.gov/homeless/hud-vash.asp.

**Supportive Services for Veterans Families (SSVF) Program:** The SSVF Program is designed to rapidly re-house homeless Veteran families and prevent homelessness for those at imminent risk due to a housing crisis. Funds are granted to private non-profit organizations and consumer cooperatives that will assist very low-income Veteran families by providing a range of supportive services designed to promote housing stability. To locate a SSVF provider in your community, please visit www.va.gov/homeless/ssvf.asp and look for the list of current year SSVF providers or call VA's National call Center for Homeless Veterans at 1-888-4AIDVET (1-888-424-3838).

**VA Benefits for Veterans Living Overseas**: VA monetary benefits, including disability compensation, pension, educational benefits, and burial allowances, are generally payable overseas. Some programs are restricted. Home loan guarantees are available only in the United States and selected U.S. territories and possessions. Educational benefits are limited to approved, degree-granting programs in institutions of higher learning. Beneficiaries living in foreign countries should contact the nearest American embassy or consulate for help. In Canada, contact an office of Veterans Affairs Canada. For information, visit www.vba.va.gov/bln/21/Foreign/index.htm.

**Incarcerated Veterans**: VA benefits are affected if a beneficiary is convicted of a felony and imprisoned for more than 60 days. Disability or death pension paid to an incarcerated beneficiary must be discontinued. Disability compensation paid to an incarcerated Veteran rated 20 percent or more disabled is limited to the 10 percent rate. For a Veteran whose disability rating is 10 percent, the payment is reduced to half of the rate payable to a Veteran evaluated as 10 percent disabled. Any amounts not paid to the Veteran while incarcerated may be apportioned to eligible dependents. Payments are not reduced for participants in work-release programs, residing in halfway houses, or under community control. Failure to notify VA of a Veteran's incarceration can result in overpayment of benefits and the subsequent loss of all VA financial benefits until the overpayment is recovered. VA benefits will not be provided to any Veteran or dependent wanted for an outstanding felony warrant.

**Health Care for Reentry Veterans Program (HCRV):** The HCRV Program offers outreach to Veterans incarcerated in state and federal prisons, and referrals and short-term case management assistance upon release from prison. The Veterans Justice Outreach Program (VJO) offers outreach and case management to Veterans involved in law enforcement encounters, overseen by treatment courts, and incarcerated in local jails. Visit www.va.gov/homeless to locate an outreach worker.

**Veterans Justice Outreach (VJO) Program:** The VJO Program offers outreach and linkage to needed treatment and services to Veterans involved in law enforcement encounters, seen in the court system, and/or incarcerated in local jails who may be at risk for homelessness upon their release.  Visit www.va.gov/HOMELESS/ VJO.asp to locate a Veterans Justice Outreach Specialist.

**Veterans of Operations Enduring Freedom, Iraqi Freedom, and New Dawn (OEF/OIF/OND):** VA has personnel stationed at major military hospitals to help seriously injured Servicemembers returning from OEF/OIF/OND as they transition from military to civilian life. OEF/OIF/OND Servicemembers who have questions about VA benefits, need assistance filing a VA claim or, or need assistance accessing services can contact the nearest VA office or call 1-800-827-1000.

**Transition Assistance Program (TAP):** TAP consists of comprehensive workshops at military installations designed to assist Servicemembers as they transition from military to civilian life. The program includes job and career search instruction, employment and training information, as well as VA benefits information for Servicemembers who are within 18 months of separation or retirement. VA benefit briefings are comprised of two briefings focusing on education, benefits, VA health care, and disability compensation. There are also optional classes for career technical training and entrepreneurship. Servicemembers can also sign up for one-on-one appointments with a VA representative; interested Servicemembers should contact their local TAP manager to sign up for this program.

**VOW to Hire Heroes Act of 2011**: The Act made TAP, including attendance at VA benefit briefings, mandatory for most Servicemembers transitioning to civilian status; upgraded career counseling options; and tailored TAP for the 21st century job market. The Act allows Servicemembers to begin the post-military employment process prior to separation or retirement from military service. This enhances opportunities to connect transitioning Servicemembers to both private-sector employers and Federal agencies seeking to hire Veterans. It also provides disabled Veterans up to one year of additional vocational rehabilitation and employment benefits.

The Act requires the Department of Labor to look at military skills and training equivalencies that are transferrable to the civilian sector, and make it easier to obtain licenses and certifications. Through the Veterans Employment Center (VEC), Servicemembers and Veterans can explore how their military skills translate into private-sector language, in order to better communicate their abilities and experiences to potential employers.

The Act provides tax credits for hiring Veterans and disabled Veterans who are out of work

**inTransition:** inTransition is a free, voluntary program with coaches who provide psychological health care support to Servicemembers, Veterans, and their health care providers during times of transition. This program provides access to transitional support, motivation, and healthy lifestyle assistance and advice from qualified coaches through the toll-free telephone number 1-800-424-7877. For more information visit http://intransition.dcoe.mil.

**Federal Recovery Coordination Program (FRCP)**: FRCP is a joint program of DoD and VA that coordinates access to federal, state, and local programs, benefits, and services for seriously wounded, ill, and injured Servicemembers, and their families through recovery, rehabilitation, and reintegration into the community.

**Pre-Separation Counseling through the Military Services**: Servicemembers may receive pre-separation counseling 24 months prior to retirement or 12 months prior to separation from active duty. These sessions present information on education, training, employment assistance, National Guard and Reserve programs, medical benefits, and financial assistance.

**Verification of Military Experience and Training (VMET)**: The VMET document, DD Form 2586, helps Servicemembers verify previous experience and training for potential employers, negotiate credits at schools, and obtain certificates or licenses. VMET documents are available through each military branch's support office and are intended for Servicemembers who have at least six months of active service. Servicemembers should obtain VMET documents from their Transition Support Office within 12 months of separation or 24 months of retirement.

**Veterans' Workforce Investment Program**: Recently separated Veterans and those with service-connected disabilities, significant barriers to employment, or who served on active duty during a period in which a campaign or expedition badge was authorized, can contact the nearest state employment office for employment help through the Veterans Workforce Investment Program. The program may be conducted through state or local public agencies, community organizations, or nonprofit organizations.

**State Employment Services**: Veterans can find employment information, education and training opportunities, job counseling, job search workshops, and resume preparation assistance at state Workforce Career or American Job Centers. These offices also have specialists to help disabled Veterans find employment.

**Unemployment Compensation**: Veterans who do not begin civilian employment immediately after leaving military service may receive weekly unemployment compensation for a limited time. The amount and duration of payments are determined by individual states. Apply by contacting the nearest state employment office listed in the local telephone directory.

**Veterans Preference for Federal Jobs**: Veterans' preference in its present form comes from the Veterans' Preference Act of 1944, as amended, and now codified in Title 5, United States Code. By law, Veterans who are disabled or who served on active duty in the U.S. Armed Forces during certain specified time periods or in military campaigns are entitled to preference over others when hiring from competitive lists of eligible candidates as well as with retention during a reduction in force. To receive preference, a Veteran must have been discharged or released from active duty in the U.S. Armed Forces under honorable conditions (honorable or general discharge). Preference is also provided for certain widows and widowers of deceased Veterans who died in service, spouses of service-connected disabled Veterans, and mothers of Veterans who died under honorable conditions on active duty or have permanent and total service-connected disabilities. For more information, visit www.fedshirevets.gov.

**Veterans' Recruitment Appointment**: This appointment allows Federal Agencies to appoint eligible Veterans to jobs without competition. These appointments can be converted to career or career-conditional positions after 2 years of satisfactory work. Veterans should apply directly to the agency where they wish to work.

**VA's Center for Veterans Enterprise**: VA's Center for Veterans Enterprise helps Veterans interested in forming or expanding small businesses, and helps VA contracting offices identify Veteran-owned small businesses. Like other Federal Agencies, VA is required to place a portion of its contracts and purchases with small and disadvantaged businesses. VA has a special office to help small and disadvantaged businesses get information on VA acquisition opportunities. For information, write to the Department of Veterans Affairs (OOSB), 810 Vermont Avenue, N.W., Washington, DC 20420-0001, call toll-free 1-800-949-8387, or visit www.va.gov/osdbu/.

**Dependents and Survivors Health Care - Civilian Health and Medical Program of the Department of Veterans Affairs (CHAMP-VA)**: Under CHAMPVA, certain dependents and survivors can receive reimbursement for most medical expenses including inpatient, outpatient, mental health, prescription medication, skilled nursing care, and durable medical equipment. To be eligible for CHAMPVA, an individual cannot be eligible for TRICARE (the medical program for civilian dependents provided by DoD) and must be one of the following:

1. The spouse or child of a Veteran whom VA has rated permanently and totally disabled due to a service-connected disability.

2. The surviving spouse or child of a Veteran who died from a VA-rated service-connected disability, or who, at the time of death,

was rated permanently and totally disabled.

3. The surviving spouse or child of a Veteran who died on active duty service and in the line of duty, not due to misconduct.

However, in most of these cases, these family members are eligible for TRICARE, not CHAMPVA. A surviving spouse under age 55 who remarries loses CHAMPVA eligibility at midnight of the date on remarriage. He/she may re-establish eligibility if the remarriage ends by death, divorce, or annulment effective the first day of the month following the termination of the remarriage or December 1, 1999, whichever is later. A surviving spouse who remarries after age 55 does not lose eligibility upon remarriage.

For those who have Medicare entitlement or other health insurance, CHAMPVA is a secondary payer. Beneficiaries with Medicare must be enrolled in Parts A and B to maintain CHAMPVA eligibility. For additional information, write to CHAMPVA, P.O. Box 469028, Denver, CO 80246, call 1-800-733-8387, or visit www.va.gov/hac/forbeneficiaries/champva/champva.asp.

**Key Information for Family Members about the Affordable Care Act**: The Affordable Care Act, also known as the Health Care Law, was created to expand access to affordable health care coverage to all Americans, lower costs, and improve quality and care coordination. Under the health care law, people will:

• Have health coverage that meets a minimum standard (called "minimum essential coverage") by Jan. 1, 2014;

• Qualify for an exemption; or

• Pay a fee when filing their taxes if they have affordable options but remain uninsured.

VA wants all Veterans and their families to receive health care that improves their health and well-being, since family members are a key part of Veterans' good health and support networks. Dependents and Survivors enrolled in CHAMPVA or the Spina Bifida Health Care Program meet the requirement to have health care coverage under the Health Care Law and do not need to take any additional steps. The law does not change CHAMPVA or Spina Bifida benefits, access, or costs. Veterans' family members who do not have coverage that meets the Health Care Law's standard should consider their options through the Health Insurance Marketplace, which is a new way to shop for and purchase private health insurance. For more information about the Health Insurance Marketplace, visit www.healthcare.gov or call 1-800-318-2596. For additional information about the VA and the health care law, visit www.va.gov/aca or call 1-877-222-VETS (8387).

**Dependents and Survivors Benefits - Death Gratuity Payment**: Military services provide payment, called a death gratuity, in the amount of $100,000 to the next of kin of Servicemembers who die while on active duty (including those who die within 120 days of separation as a result of service-connected injury or illness). If there is no surviving spouse or child, then parents or siblings designated as next of kin by the Servicemember may be provided the payment. The payment is made by the last military command of the deceased. If the beneficiary is not paid automatically, application may be made to the military service concerned.

**Dependents and Survivors Benefits - Dependency and Indemnity Compensation (DIC)**: DIC is a tax-free monetary benefit paid to eligible Survivors of military Servicemembers who died in the line of duty or eligible survivors of Veterans whose death resulted from a service-related injury or disease. DIC may also be paid to certain Survivors of Veterans who were totally disabled from service-connected conditions at the time of death, even though their service-connected disabilities did not cause their deaths. The survivor qualifies if the Veteran was:

- Continuously rated totally disabled for a period of 10 years immediately preceding death; or

- Continuously rated totally disabled from the date of military discharge and for at least 5 years immediately preceding death; or

- A former POW who was continuously rated totally disabled for a period of at least one year immediately preceding death.

For more detailed information, visit www.benefits.va.gov/COMPENSATION/current_rates_DIC.asp.

**DIC Eligibility (Surviving Spouse)**: To qualify for DIC, a surviving spouse must meet the requirements below:

* Married to a Servicemember who died on active duty, active duty for training, or inactive duty training, OR

* Validly married the Veteran before January 1, 1957, OR

* Married the Veteran within 15 years of discharge from the period of military service in which the disease or injury that caused the Veteran's death began or was aggravated, OR

* Was married to the Veteran for at least one year, OR

* Had a child with the Veteran, AND

* Cohabitated with the Veteran continuously until the Veteran's death, or if separated, was not at fault for the separation, AND

* Is not currently remarried

  Note: A surviving spouse who remarries on or after December 16, 2003, and on or after attaining age 57, is entitled to continue to receive DIC.

Payments will be offset by any amount received from judicial proceedings brought on by the Veteran's death. When the surviving spouse is eligible for payments under the military's Survivor Benefit Plan (SBP), only the amount of SBP greater than DIC is payable. If DIC is greater than SBP, only DIC is payable.

**DIC Eligibility (Surviving Child)**: Not included on the surviving spouse's DIC, AND:
* Unmarried, AND

* Under age 18, or between the ages of 18 and 23 and attending school.

Note: A child adopted out of the Veteran's family may be eligible for DIC if all other eligibility criteria are met.

**DIC Eligibility (Surviving Parent):** Parents' DIC is a tax-free, income-based, monthly benefit for the parent(s) of a Servicemember who died in the line of duty or a Veteran whose death resulted from a service-related injury or disease. The surviving parent(s) must have an income below a limit established by law. The term "parent" includes:

- Biological

- Adoptive

- Foster parents (A foster parent is a person who stood in the relationship of a parent to the Veteran for at least one year before the Veteran's last entry into active service.)

**DIC and Aid and Attendance/Housebound Benefits**: Surviving spouses of Veterans who died on or after Jan. 1, 1993, may receive additional benefits for aid and attendance if they are patients in a nursing home or require the regular assistance of another person, or if they are permanently housebound.

**DIC 8-Year Kicker Special Allowance**: If the Veteran was totally disabled 8 continuous years prior to death, an additional special allowance of $261.87 will be added to the monthly DIC award. If there are dependent children under age 18, an additional $266.00 will be added for the initial 2 years of entitlement for DIC awards commencing on or after Jan. 1, 2005.

**Restored Entitlement Program for Survivors**: Survivors of Veterans who died of service-connected causes incurred or aggravated prior to Aug. 13, 1981, may be eligible for a special benefit payable in addition to any other benefits to which the family may be entitled. The amount of the benefit is based on information provided by the Social Security Administration.

**Survivors Pension**: Survivors pension is a tax-free monetary benefit payable to a low-income, unremarried surviving spouses and/or unmarried child(ren) of a deceased Veteran with wartime service. Survivors pension is based on yearly family income, which must be less than the amount set by Congress to qualify. Survivors pension provides a monthly payment to bring an eligible person's income to a level established by law. The payment is reduced by the annual income from other sources, such as Social Security. The payment may be increased if the recipient has unreimbursed medical expenses that can be deducted from countable income.

To be eligible, the deceased Veteran must have met the following service requirements:

- For service on or before Sept. 7, 1980, the Veteran must have served at least 90 days of active military service, with at least one day during a war time period.

- If the Veteran entered active duty after Sept.7, 1980, generally the Veteran must have served at least 24 months or the full period for which called or ordered to active duty with at least one day during a war time period.

- Was discharged from service under other than dishonorable conditions

While an unremarried spouse is eligible at any age, a child of a deceased wartime Veteran must be:

- Under 18, OR

- Under 23 if attending a VA-approved school, OR

- Permanently incapable of self-support due to a disability before age 18

**Survivors Aid and Attendance and Housebound Benefits**: Survivors who are eligible for pension and require the aid and attendance of another person, or are housebound, may be eligible for a higher maximum pension rate. These benefits cannot be paid without eligibility to pension. Since aid and attendance and housebound allowances increase the pension amount, people who are not eligible for a basic pension due to excessive income may be eligible for pension at these increased rates. A surviving spouse may not receive aid and attendance benefits and housebound benefits at the same time.

To apply for aid and attendance or housebound benefits, write to a VA regional office. Please include copies of any evidence, preferably a report from an attending physician or a nursing home, validating the need for aid and attendance or housebound type care.

The report should contain sufficient detail to determine whether there is disease or injury producing physical or mental impairment, loss of coordination, or conditions affecting the ability to dress and undress, to feed oneself, to attend to sanitary needs, and to keep oneself ordinarily clean and presentable. In addition, it is necessary to determine whether the claimant is confined to the home or immediate premises.

**Survivors' & Dependents' Educational Assistance (DEA)**: VA provides educational assistance to qualifying dependents for pursuit of associate, bachelor, or graduate degrees at colleges and universities; independent study; cooperative training; study abroad; certificate or diploma from business, technical, or vocational schools; apprenticeships; on-the-job training programs; farm cooperative courses; and preparatory courses for tests required or used for admission to an institution of higher learning or graduate school. Beneficiaries without high-school degrees can pursue secondary schooling, and those with a deficiency in a subject may receive tutorial assistance if enrolled half-time or more.

**Eligible dependents include:**
- The spouse or child of a Servicemember or Veteran who either died of a service-connected disability, or who has permanent and total service-connected disability, or who died while such a disability existed.

- The spouse or child of a Servicemember currently listed for more than 90 days as MIA, captured in the line of duty by a hostile force, or detained or interned by a foreign government or power.

- The spouse or child of a Servicemember who is hospitalized or receives outpatient care or treatment for a disability that is determined to be totally and permanently disabling, incurred or aggravated due to active duty, and for which the Servicemember is likely to be discharged from military service.

The period of eligibility for Veterans' spouses expires 10 years from either the date they become eligible or the date of the Veteran's death. Children generally must be between the ages of 18 and 26 to receive educational benefits. VA may grant extensions to both spouses and children. The period of eligibility for spouses of Servicemembers who died on active duty expires 20 years from the date of death. If the spouse's marriage to the Veteran ends in divorce, eligibility for DEA benefits ends on that date. Dependent children do not lose eligibility if they marry.

Dependents over age 14 with physical or mental disabilities that impair their ability to pursue an education may receive specialized vocational or restorative training, including speech and voice correction, language retraining, lip reading, auditory training, Braille reading and writing, and similar programs. Certain disabled or surviving spouses are also eligible.

**Children of Women Vietnam Veterans Born with Certain Birth Defects:** Biological children of women Veterans who served in Vietnam at any time during the period beginning on Feb. 28, 1961, and ending on May 7, 1975, may be eligible for certain benefits because of birth defects associated with the mother's service in Vietnam that resulted in a permanent physical or mental disability. The covered birth defects do not include conditions due to family disorders, birth-related injuries, or fetal or neonatal infirmities with well-established causes. A monetary allowance is paid at one of four disability levels based on the child's degree of permanent disability.

**Appeals of VA Claims Decisions**: Veterans and other claimants for VA benefits have the right to appeal decisions made by a VA regional office, medical center, or National Cemetery Administration office. Typical issues appealed are disability compensation, pension, education benefits, recovery of overpayments, reimbursement for unauthorized medical services, and denial of burial and memorial benefits. A claimant has one year from the date of the notification of a VA decision to file an appeal. The first step in the appeal process is for a claimant to file a written notice of disagreement with the VA office that made the decision.

Following receipt of the written notice, VA will furnish the claimant a "statement of the case" describing what facts, laws, and regulations were used in deciding the case. To complete the request for appeal, the claimant must file a "substantive appeal" within 60 days of the mailing of the statement of the case, or within one year from the date VA mailed its decision, whichever period ends later.

**Board of Veterans' Appeals:** The Board of Veterans' Appeals ("the Board") makes decisions on appeals on behalf of the Secretary of Veterans Affairs. Although it is not required, a Veterans Service Organization, an agent, or an attorney may represent a claimant. Appellants may present their cases in person to a member of the Board at a hearing in Washington, D.C., at a VA regional office, or by video-conference. Decisions made by the Board can be found at <u>www.</u>

index.va.gov/search/va/bva.html. The pamphlet, "Understanding the Appeal Process," is available on the website or may be requested by writing to Mail Process Section (014), Board of Veterans' Appeals, 810 Vermont Avenue, N.W., Washington, DC 20420.

**U.S. Court of Appeals for Veterans Claims:** A final Board of Veterans' Appeals decision that does not grant a claimant the benefits desired may be appealed to the U.S. Court of Appeals for Veterans Claims. The court is an independent body, and is not part of the Department of Veterans Affairs. Notice of an appeal must be received by the court with a postmark that is within 120 days after the Board of Veterans' Appeals mailed its decision.

The court reviews the record considered by the Board of Veterans' Appeals. It does not hold trials or receive new evidence. Appellants may represent themselves before the court or have lawyers or approved agents as representatives. Oral argument is held only at the direction of the court. Either party may appeal a decision of the court to the U.S. Court of Appeals for the Federal Circuit and may seek review in the Supreme Court of the United States. Published decisions, case status information, rules and procedures, and other special announcements can be found at www.uscourts.cavc.gov/. The court's decisions can also be found in West's Veterans Appeals Reporter, and on the Westlaw and LEXIS online services. For questions, write the Clerk of the Court, 625 Indiana Avenue, N.W., Suite 900, Washington, DC 20004, or call (202) 501-5970

**Replacement Military Medals and Records**: Medals awarded while in active service are replaced by the individual military services, if requested by Veterans or their next of kin. Requests for replacement medals, decorations, and awards should be directed to the branch of the military in which the Veteran served. However, for Air Force (including Army Air Corps) and Army Veterans, the National Personnel Records Center (NPRC) verifies awards and forwards requests and verification to appropriate services.

Requests for replacement medals should be submitted on Standard Form 180, "Request Pertaining to Military Records," which may be obtained at VA offices or at www.va.gov/vaforms. Forms, addresses, and other information on requesting medals can be found on the Military Personnel Records section of NPRC's Website at www.archives.gov/st-louis/military-personnel/index.html. For questions, call Military

Personnel Records at (314) 801-0800, or email questions to MPR. center@nara.gov.

When requesting medals include the Veteran's full name, branch of service, service number or Social Security number, and exact or approximate dates of military service. The request must contain the signature of the Veteran, or the next of kin if the Veteran is deceased.

If available, include a copy of the discharge or separation document, WDAGO Form 53-55 or DD Form 214. If discharge or separation documents are lost, Veterans or the next of kin of deceased Veterans may obtain duplicate copies through the eBenefits portal (www. ebenefits.va.gov) or by completing Standard Form 180, Request Pertaining to Military Records, found at www.archives.gov/research/index.html or by writing to the NPRC Military Personnel Records, One Archives Drive, St. Louis, MO 63138-1002, and specify that a duplicate separation document is needed.

**Correcting Military Records**: The Secretary of a military department, acting through a Board for Correction of Military Records, has authority to change any military record when necessary to correct an error or remove an injustice. A correction board may consider applications for correction of a military record, including a review of a discharge issued by court-martial. Application is made with DD Form 149, available at VA offices, Veterans Service Organizations or visit www.dtic.mil/whs/directives/infomgt/forms/formsprogram.htm.

**Review of Discharge from Military Service**: Veterans with disabilities incurred or aggravated during active duty may qualify for medical or related benefits regardless of the type of separation or discharge and characterization of service. Veterans separated administratively under other than honorable conditions may request that their discharge be reviewed for possible re-characterization, provided they file their appeal within 15 years of the date of separation.

Each of the military services maintains a discharge review board with authority to change, correct, or modify discharges or dismissals not issued by a sentence of a general court-martial. The board has no authority to address medical discharges. If the Veteran is deceased or incompetent, the surviving spouse, next of kin, or legal representative may apply for a review of discharge by writing to the military department concerned, using DD Form 293, "Application for the

Review of Discharge from the Armed Forces of the United States." This form may be obtained at a VA regional office, from veterans organizations or online at www.dtic.mil/whs/directives/infomgt/forms/formsprogram.htm. Questions regarding the review of a discharge should be addressed to the appropriate discharge review board at the address listed on the DD Form 293.

If the discharge was more than 15 years ago, a Veteran must petition the appropriate Service's Board for Correction of Military Records using DD Form 149, "Application for Correction of Military Records Under the Provisions of Title 10, U.S. Code, Section 1552." A discharge review is conducted by a review of an applicant's record and, if requested, by a hearing before the board.

Discharges awarded as a result of a continuous period of unauthorized absence in excess of 180 days make persons ineligible for VA benefits regardless of action taken by discharge review boards, unless VA determines there were compelling circumstances for the absence. Boards for the Correction of Military Records also may consider such cases.

**Physical Disability Board of Review:** Veterans separated due to disability from Sept. 11, 2001, through Dec. 31, 2009, with a combined rating of 20 percent or less, as determined by the respective branch of service Physical Evaluation Board (PEB), and not found eligible for retirement, may be eligible for a review by the Physical Disability Board of Review (PDBR). The PDBR was established to reassess the accuracy and fairness of certain PEB decisions, and where appropriate, recommend the correction of discrepancies and errors.

A PDBR review will not lower the disability rating previously assigned by the PEB, and any correction may be made retroactively to the day of the original disability separation. As a result of the request for review by the PDBR, no further relief from the Board of Corrections of Military Records may be sought, and the recommendation by the PDBR, once accepted by the respective branch of service, is final. A comparison of these two boards, along with other PDBR information, can be viewed at www.health.mil/pdbr. Questions regarding the review of a discharge should be addressed to the appropriate discharge review board at the address listed on the DD Form 293.

**Low Income Home Energy Assistance Program (LIHEAP):** The U.S. Department of Health and Human Services provides funding to states to help low-income households with their heating and home energy costs under the LIHEAP. The LIHEAP can also assist with insulating homes to make them more energy efficient and reduce energy costs. The LIHEAP in the Veteran's community determines if their household's income qualifies for the program. To find out where to apply call 1-866-674-6327 or e-mail energy@ncat.org. More information can be found at www.acf.hhs.gov/programs/ocs/liheap/#index.html.

## Federal Recovery Coordination Program

The Federal Recovery Coordination Program (FRCP), a joint program of DoD and VA assists severely wounded, ill, or injured Service members, Veterans, and their families navigate, coordinate, and access healthcare, services, and benefits provided by DoD, VA, other federal agencies, state, and private organizations.

The Federal Recovery Coordinators (FRCs) provide personalized assistance to Service members and Veterans with complex care coordination needs. Service members or Veterans may benefit from FRCP care coordination if they: a) have been diagnosed with one or more acute conditions; b) have a high potential for life-long care; or c) need assistance with advocacy and navigating VA or DoD healthcare and benefits.

To make a referral to the program or get more information please visit www.va.gov/icbc/frcp

# Burial and Memorial Benefits

Burial in a VA national cemetery is open to all members of the armed forces and Veterans who have met minimum active duty service requirements and were discharged under conditions other than dishonorable. Members of the reserve components of the armed forces who die while on active duty or while performing training duty or who have 20 years of service creditable for retired pay, or were called to active duty by executive federal order and served the full term of service may also be eligible for burial. The Veterans' spouse, minor children and under certain conditions dependent unmarried adult children may be eligible for burial even if they predecease the Veteran.

## Burial in VA National Cemeteries

Burial in a VA national cemetery is available at no cost and includes the gravesite, grave-liner, opening and closing of the grave, a headstone or marker, and perpetual care as part of a national shrine. For Veterans and Servicemembers, benefits may also include a burial flag, Presidential Memorial Certificate (PMC) and military funeral honors provided by the Department of Defense.

With certain exceptions, active duty service beginning after Sep. 7, 1980, as an enlisted person, and after Oct 16, 1981, as an officer, must be for a minimum of 24 consecutive months or the full period of active duty (as in the case of reservists or National Guard members called to active duty for a limited duration by executive Federal order). Active duty for training, by itself, while serving in the reserves or National Guard, is not sufficient to confer eligibility; however, circumstances surrounding the death of a Servicemember while in training may influence eligibility for burial or memorial benefits. Reservists and National Guard members, as well as their spouses and dependent children, are eligible if they were entitled to retired pay at the time of death, or would have been upon reaching requisite age.

Eligible individuals found to have committed federal or state capital crimes or certain sex offenses are barred from burial in a VA national cemetery and from receipt of a Government-furnished headstone, marker, medallion, burial flag, and Presidential Memorial Certificate. Veterans and other claimants for VA burial benefits have the right to appeal decisions made by VA regarding eligibility for burial in a VA national cemetery or other memorial benefits. Chapter 13 discusses the procedures for appealing VA claims. This chapter contains information on the full range of VA burial and memorial benefits. Readers with questions may contact the nearest VA national cemetery, listed by state in the VA Facilities section of this book; call 1-800-827-1000; or visit the web site at www.cem.va.gov/.

Surviving spouses of Veterans who died on or after Jan. 1, 2000, do not lose eligibility for burial in a VA national cemetery if they remarry. Unmarried dependent children of Veterans who are under 21 years of age, or under 23 years of age if a full-time student at an approved educational institution, are eligible for burial. Unmarried adult children who become physically or mentally disabled and incapable of self-support before age 21, or age 23 if a full-time student, may also be eligible.

Certain parents of Servicemembers who die as a result of hostile activity or from combat training-related injuries may be eligible for burial in a VA national cemetery with their child. The biological or adopted parents of a Servicemember who died in combat or while performing training in preparation for a combat mission, who leaves no surviving spouse or dependent child, may be buried with the deceased Servicemember if there is available space. Eligibility is limited to Servicemembers who died on or after Oct. 7, 2001, and biological or adoptive parents who died on or after Oct. 13, 2010.

VA is establishing a formal Pre-Need program that provides a determination of eligibility for burial in a VA national cemetery in advance of need. This program will provide an opportunity for individuals to learn if they are eligible for burial in a VA national cemetery and the ability to communicate their final wishes to loved ones and funeral service providers.

If the individual is deceased, the next of kin or authorized representative (e.g., funeral director) should contact the National Cemetery Scheduling Office to schedule a burial (see information available at www.cem.va.gov/cem/burial_benefits/need.asp). VA normally does not conduct burials on weekends. Gravesites are assigned at the time VA receives a request for burial at a national cemetery with available space and cannot be reserved in advance.

The National Cemetery Scheduling Office verifies eligibility for burial. A copy of the Veteran's discharge document that specifies the period(s) of active duty and character of service is usually sufficient to determine eligibility. A copy of the deceased's death certificate and proof of relationship to the Veteran (for eligible family members) may be required.

VA operates 134 VA national cemeteries, of which 76 are currently open for both new casket and cremation interments and 17 may accept new interment of cremated remains only. Burial options are limited to those available at a specific cemetery and may include inground casketed gravesite, or interment of cremated remains in a columbarium niche, in-ground gravesite, or in a scattering area. Contact the National Cemetery Scheduling Office or a VA national cemetery directly, or visit our website at http://www.cem.va.gov to determine whether a particular cemetery is open for new burials, and what other options are available.

## Headstones, Markers and Medallions

Veterans, active duty Servicemembers, retired Reservists and National Guard members, and Reservists and National Guard members with creditable active duty service, are eligible for an inscribed headstone or marker for their unmarked gravesite at any national, state Veterans, tribal, or private cemetery. VA will deliver a headstone or marker at no cost, anywhere in the world.

For eligible Veterans or Servicemembers buried in a private cemetery whose deaths occurred on or after Nov. 1, 1990, VA may provide a Government-furnished headstone or marker (even if the grave is already marked with a private one); or VA may furnish a medallion to affix to an existing privately-purchased headstone or marker.

Spouses and dependent children are eligible for a Government-furnished headstone or marker only if they are buried in a VA national or state or tribal Veterans cemetery and their death occurs prior to the Veteran's death. After the Veteran's death, their inscription will share the Government-furnished headstone or marker.

Flat markers are available in bronze, granite or marble. Upright headstones come in granite or marble. The style provided will be consistent with existing monuments at the place of burial. Niche markers are available to mark columbarium niches used for inurnment of cremated remains. Medallions are made of bronze and are available in three sizes: Large, 5-inch ( 6 3/8" W x 4 ¾" H x ½" D), Medium, 3-inch ( 3 ¾" W x 2 7/8" H x ¼" D) and Small, 1 ½-inch (2" W x 1 ½" H x 1/3" D). Headstones, markers and medallions previously furnished by the Government may be replaced at Government expense if badly deteriorated, illegible, vandalized or stolen.

Headstones or markers for VA national cemeteries will be ordered by the cemetery director using information provided by the individual making burial arrangements or the authorized representative. Before ordering a headstone or marker for placement in a private cemetery, the applicant or authorized representative should check with the cemetery to ensure that the type of Government-furnished headstone or marker will be appropriate for the burial section within their cemetery. All installation fees at private cemeteries are the responsibility of the applicant.

To submit a claim for a headstone or marker for a gravesite in a private cemetery, use VA Form 40-1330, Application for Standard Government Headstone or Marker (available at http://www.va.gov/vaforms/. A copy of the Veteran's military discharge document is required for processing. Mail forms to Memorial Programs Service, Department of Veterans Affairs, 5109 Russell Road, Quantico, VA 22134-3903. The form and supporting documents may also be faxed toll free to 1-800-455-7143.

**"In Memory Of" Markers:** VA provides memorial headstones and markers with "In Memory Of" as the first line of inscription for those whose remains have not been recovered or identified, were buried at sea, donated to science or cremated and scattered.

Eligibility is the same as for regular headstones and markers. There is no fee when the "In Memory Of" marker is placed in a VA national cemetery. All installation fees at private cemeteries are the responsibility of the applicant. Memorial headstones and markers for spouses and dependents may only be provided for placement in a VA national or state or tribal Veterans cemetery.

**Inscriptions:** The mandatory inscription for headstones and markers must include the full name of the deceased, branch of service, and year of birth and death. They also may be inscribed with other optional information, including an emblem of belief; military rank; war service such as "World War II;" complete dates of birth and death; military awards; and military units or organizations. Space permitting, additional inscriptions may also be included such as civilian or Veteran affiliations; and personalized words of endearment.

**Medallion in lieu of government headstone or marker for private cemeteries:** For Veterans or Servicemembers whose death occurred on or after Nov. 1, 1990, VA is authorized to provide a medallion instead of a headstone or marker if the gravesite is in a private cemetery and already marked with a privately-purchased headstone or marker.

To submit a claim for a medallion to be affixed to a private headstone/marker in a private cemetery, use VA Form 40-1330M, Claim for Government Medallion (available at http://www.va.gov/vaforms). A copy of the Veteran's military discharge document is required. Mail forms to Memorial Programs Service, Department of Veterans Affairs, 5109 Russell Road, Quantico, VA 22134-3903. The form and supporting documents may also be faxed toll free to 1-800-455-7143.

To check the status of a claim for a headstone or marker for placement in a VA national, state or tribal Veterans cemetery, please call the cemetery.

To check the status of a headstone or marker to be placed in a private cemetery, please contact the Applicant Assistance Unit at 1-800-697-6947, or via email at mps.headstones@va.gov.

### Other Memorialization

**Presidential Memorial Certificates:** Presidential Memorial Certificates are issued to recognize the military service of honorably discharged deceased Veterans and persons who died in the active military, naval, or air service. Next of kin, relatives and other loved ones may apply for a certificate by mailing or faxing a completed and signed VA Form 40-0247, Presidential Memorial Certificate Request Form (available at http://www.va.gov/vaforms), along with a copy of the Veteran's military discharge documents or proof of honorable military service. The processing of requests sent without supporting documents will be delayed until eligibility can be determined. Eligibility requirements can be found at http://www.cem.va.gov.

**Burial Flags:** Generally, VA will furnish one U.S. burial flag to memorialize each Veteran who received an other than dishonorable discharge. This includes certain persons who served in the organized military forces of the Commonwealth of the Philippines while in service of the U.S armed forces and who died on or after April 25, 1951. Also eligible for a burial flag are Veterans who were entitled to retired pay for service in the Reserve or National Guard, or would have been entitled if over age 60; and members or former members of the Selected Reserve who served their initial obligation, or were discharged for a disability incurred or aggravated in the line of duty, or died while a member of the Selected Reserve. The applicant may apply for the flag at any VA Regional Office or U.S. Post Office by completing VA Form 21-2008, Application for United States Flag for Burial Purposes (available at http://www.va.gov/vaforms/. In most cases, a funeral director will help the family obtain the flag.

**Reimbursement of Burial Expenses:** VA will pay a burial allowance up to $2,000 if the Veteran's death is service-connected. In such cases, the person who bore the Veteran's burial expenses may claim reimbursement from VA.

In some cases, VA will pay the cost of transporting the remains of a Veteran whose death was service-connected to the nearest VA national cemetery with available gravesites. There is no time limit for filing reimbursement claims in service-connected death cases.

**Unclaimed Remains of Veterans:** "Unclaimed Veterans" are defined as those who die with no next of kin to claim their remains and insufficient funds to cover burial expenses. A VA pension or other compensation is no longer a pre-requisite for these "Unclaimed Veterans" to receive monetary burial benefits. In addition to burial in a VA national, state or tribal Veterans cemetery and a government-furnished headstone or marker, there are monetary benefits associated with burial of unclaimed Veterans remains. These monetary benefits may include reimbursement for the cost of the casket or urn used for burial in a VA national cemetery, reimbursement for transportation to a VA national cemetery, a burial allowance and a plot allowance if burial is in a state, tribal or private cemetery. More information on burial benefits for Unclaimed Veterans can be found at http://www.cem.va.gov/cem/docs/factsheets/CasketUrn_Reimbursement.pdf. For Veterans who die while at a VA facility under authorized VA admission or at a non-VA facility under authorized VA admission, and whose remains are unclaimed, the closest VA healthcare facility is responsible for arranging proper burial.

**Casket or Urn Reimbursement:** The U.S. Department of Veterans Affairs (VA) will reimburse the cost of a casket or urn used to inter an Unclaimed Veteran in a VA national cemetery, who died on or after January 10, 2014, and was interred on or after May 13, 2015. The individual or entity that pays for a casket or urn may be reimbursed the actual cost of a casket or urn, not to exceed an annually established average cost. The reimbursement payable in calendar year 2015 is $1,967 for a casket and $172 for an urn. The reimbursement amount will be adjusted for inflation annually.

Applicants must submit VA Form 40-10088, Request for Reimbursement of Casket/Urn. Part I should be submitted with documentation of qualifying military service to the National Cemetery Scheduling Office (NCSO). Part I may be faxed (toll-free) to 1-866-900-6417; emailed to nca.scheduling@va.gov; or mailed to PO Box 510543, St. Louis, MO 63151. Applicants (who may differ from the individual or entity that requested burial), must submit Part II of VA Form 40-10088 with the required reimbursement documentation to NCSO at the time of the burial request, OR to the VA national cemetery before the actual interment. More information is available in the fact sheet "Unclaimed Veteran Remains Casket or Urn Reimbursement Program" located at http://www.cem.va.gov/cem/docs/factsheets/CasketUrn_Reimbursement.pdf.

**Burial Allowance:** VA will pay a burial and funeral allowance of up to $2,000 for Veterans who die from service-connected injuries. VA will pay a burial and funeral allowance of up to $300 for Veterans who, at the time of death from nonservice-connected injuries were entitled to receive pension or compensation or would have been entitled if they were not receiving military retirement pay. VA will pay a burial and funeral allowance of up to $734 when the Veteran's death occurs in a VA facility, a VA-contracted nursing home or a state Veterans nursing home. In cases in which the Veteran's death was not service connected, claims must be filed within two years after burial or cremation.

**Plot Allowance:** VA will pay a plot allowance of up to $734 when a Veteran is buried in a cemetery not under U.S. government jurisdiction if: the Veteran was discharged from active duty because of disability incurred or aggravated in the line of duty; the Veteran was receiving compensation or pension or would have been if the Veteran was not receiving military retired pay; or the Veteran died in a VA facility. The plot allowance may be paid to the state for the cost of a plot or interment in a state-owned cemetery reserved solely for Veteran burials if the Veteran is buried without charge. Burial expenses paid by the deceased's employer or a state agency will not be reimbursed.

## Veterans Cemeteries Administered by Other Agencies:

**Department of the Army:** Administers Arlington National Cemetery and other Army installation cemeteries. Eligibility is generally more restrictive than at VA national cemeteries. For information, call (703) 607-8000, write Superintendent, Arlington National Cemetery, Arlington, VA 22211, or visit www.arlingtoncemetery.mil/.

**Department of the Interior:** Administers two active national cemeteries which are Andersonville National Cemetery in Georgia, and Andrew Johnson National Cemetery in Tennessee. Eligibility is similar to VA national cemeteries. For information, call (202) 208-4747, or write: Department of Interior, National Park Service 1849 C. St. NW, Washington, D.C. 20240.

**State and Tribal Veterans Cemeteries:** There are currently 97 VA grant-funded Veterans cemeteries operating in 47 states and U.S. Territories that offer burial options for Veterans and their eligible dependents. Five of these cemeteries are operated by federally recognized tribal organizations. VA grant-funded cemeteries have similar eligibility requirements and certain states/tribal organizations may require state or tribal residency/membership. Some services, particularly for family members, may require a fee. Contact the state or tribal Veterans cemetery or the state Veterans Affairs office for information. To locate a state or tribal Veterans cemetery, visit www.cem.va.gov/grants/veterans_cemeteries.asp.

**Military Funeral Honors:** Upon request, the Department of Defense (DoD) may provide military funeral honors consisting of folding and presenting the United States flag and the playing of

"Taps." A funeral honors detail consists of two or more uniformed members of the Armed Forces, with at least one member from the deceased's branch of service.

Family members should inform their funeral director if they want military funeral honors. DoD maintains a toll-free number (1-877-MILHONR) for use by funeral directors only to request honors. VA may help arrange honors for burials at VA national cemeteries. Veterans service organizations or volunteer groups may help provide honors. For more information, visit www.military-funeralhonors.osd.mil/.